THE AWESOME ACTIVITY BOOK FOR CURIOUS KIDS

MORE THAN 300 EXERCISES THAT TEACH NUMBERS, LETTERS, COLORS, AND MORE!

THE AWESOME ACTIVITY BOOK FOR CURIOUS KIDS

MORE THAN 300 EXERCISES That Teach Numbers, Letters, Colors, and More!

Susan Shaw-Russell

FOR YOUNG READERS

Racehorse for Young Readers books may be purchased in bulk at special discounts for sales promotion, corporate gifts, fund-raising, or educational purposes. Special editions can also be created to specifications. For details, contact the Special Sales Department, Skyhorse Publishing, 307 West 36th Street, 11th Floor, New York, NY 10018 or info@skyhorsepublishing.com.

Racehorse for Young Readers™ is a pending trademark of Skyhorse Publishing, Inc.®, a Delaware corporation.

Visit our website at www.skyhorsepublishing.com.

10 9 8 7 6 5 4 3 2 1

Library of Congress Control Number: 2019912317

Cover design by Kai Texel

Cover and interior artwork by Susan Shaw-Russell

ISBN: 978-1-63158-397-1

Printed in the United States of America

FOLLOW ME

Trace the lines from left to right.

Pre-Writing Skills

INTO OUTER SPACE

Follow the rocketship from earth to outer space. Trace the path.

THROUGH THE GROUND

Help the ant get home to his friend.
Trace a path.

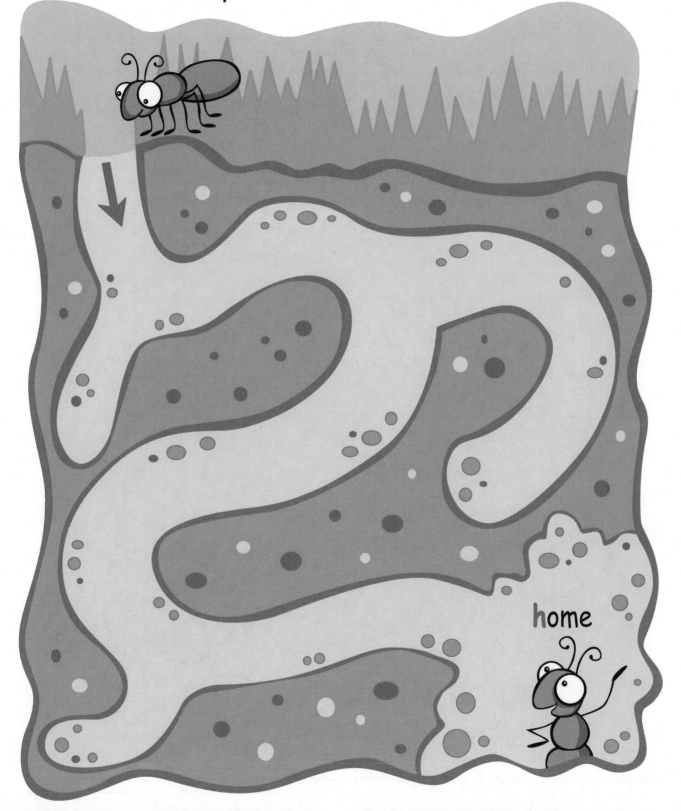

Pre-Writing Skills

WHERE DOES THE BEAR LIVE?

Help the bear find his way to his cave.
Trace a path.

CHEESE MAZE

Help the mouse get to the cheese.
Trace a path.

cheese

Pre-Writing Skills

WHAT FLIES IN THE SKY AND STARTS WITH THE LETTER k?

Trace the path from the cat's paw along the string to the kite.

kite

WHERE DO SOME FROGS LIVE?

Trace the path of the frog to his home in the pond.

pond

Pre-Writing Skills

I'M THE GINGERBREAD MAN

Help the gingerbread man down the path to his house.
Trace a path.

ON THE OPEN SEA

Lead the pirate to his treasure.
Trace a path.

treasure

Pre-Writing Skills

WHERE DOES A DINOSAUR LAY HER EGGS?

Help the dinosaur find her nest.
Trace a path.

nest

HERDING THE SHEEP

Lead the sheep to their pen at the top of the page. Trace a line.

INSIDE THE BEE HIVE

Help the bee get to his Queen in the center of the maze.

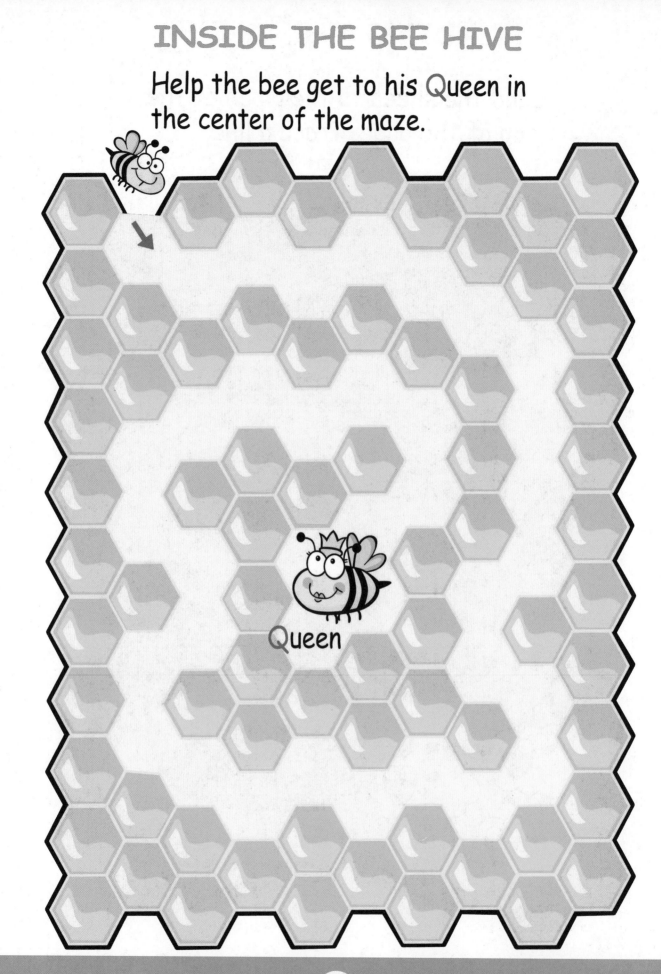

Queen

WAIT FOR ME!

Help the one fish to catch up to the group of fish called a **s**chool.

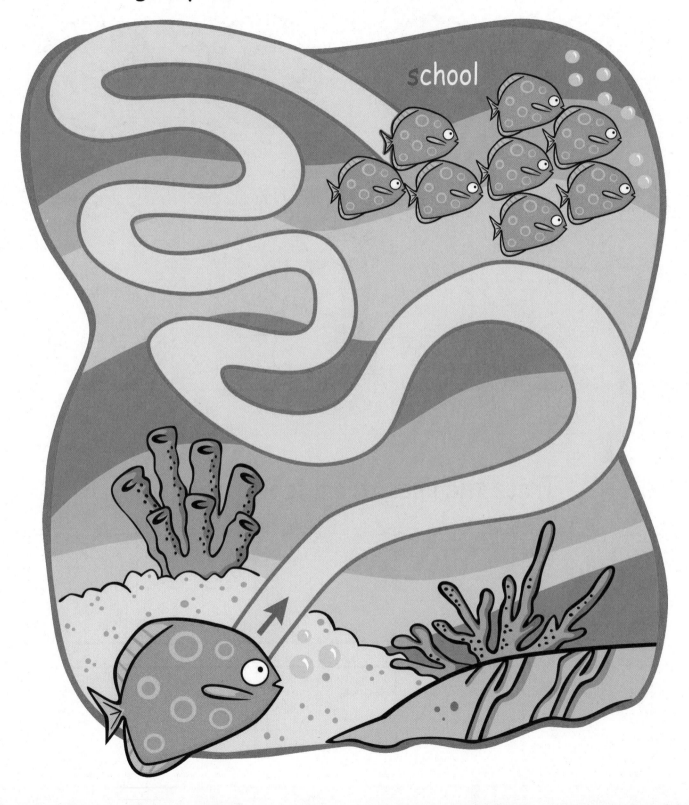

school

Pre-Writing Skills

FROM TOP TO BOTTOM

Trace the balloon string from top to bottom.

Trace the lines from top to bottom.

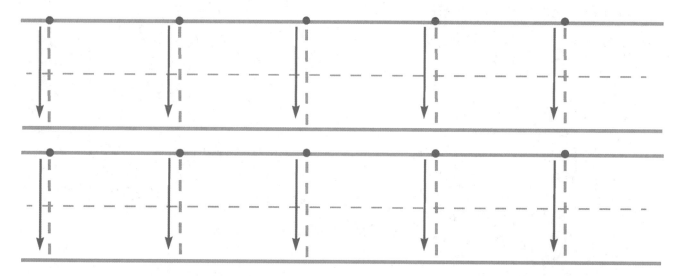

LET'S CATCH SOME FISH

Help the penguins catch some fish.
Trace their fishing lines from top to bottom.

Pre-Writing Skills

SLANTED LINES

Trace the slanted lines starting from the red dots.

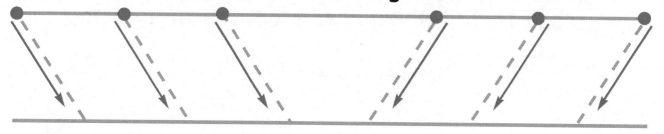

Trace the slanted lines starting from the red dots at the top of the pencils.

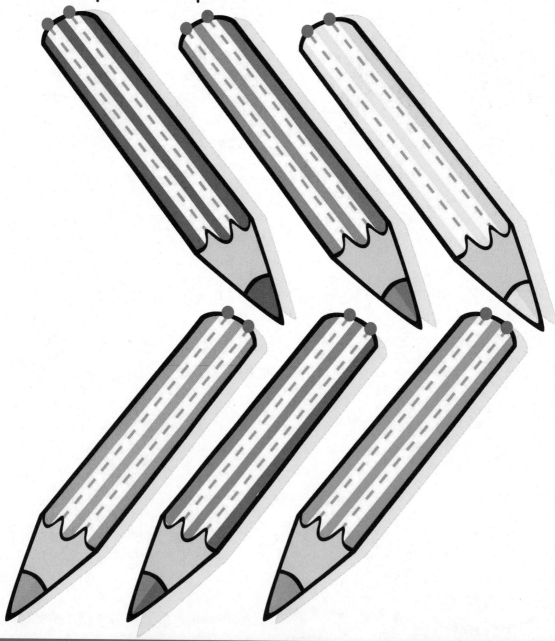

THE SNAKE CHARMER'S BASKET

Finish the weave of the snake's basket.
Trace the slanted lines starting from the red dots.

TRACE THE CURVES

Trace the curved lines on the happy faces from left to right.

Trace the curved lines below from left to right.

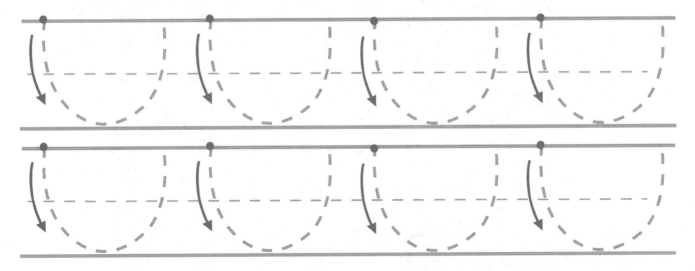

TEA FOR TWO

Trace the curved lines on the tea pot
and tea cups from left to right.

YUMMY COOKIES

Trace the circles.

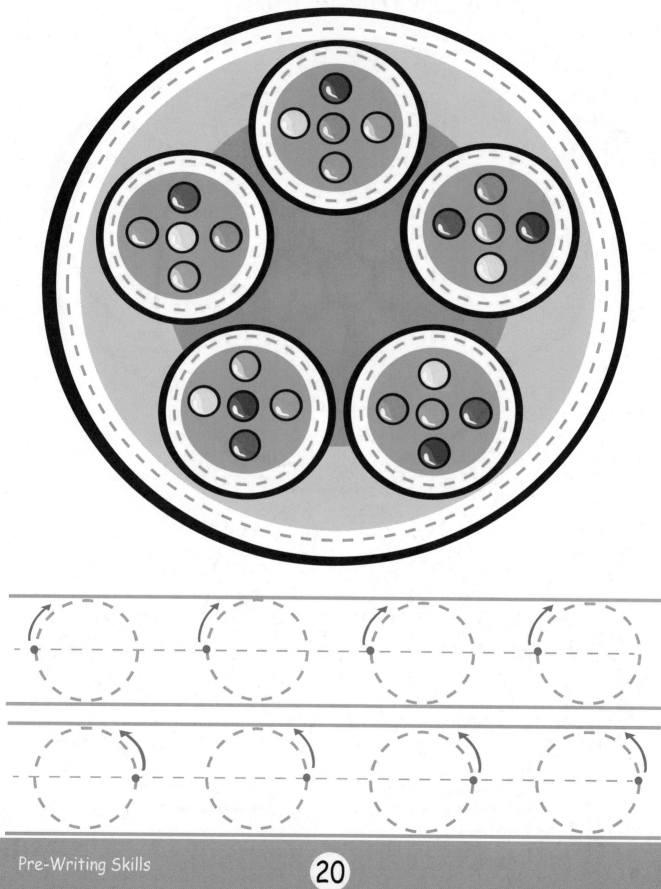

HERE'S LOOKING AT YOU!

Trace the circles to finish the alien's eyes.

Pre-Writing Skills

THIS IS THE COLOR BLUE

Color the  blue.

BLUE WHALE

THIS IS THE COLOR PURPLE

Color the  purple.

PURPLE GRAPES

Color the  yellow.

YELLOW SUN

THIS IS THE COLOR ORANGE

Color the  orange.

ORANGE PUMPKIN

THIS IS THE COLOR GREEN

Color the  green.

GREEN TURTLE

THIS IS THE COLOR RED

Color the  red.

RED CRAB

THIS IS THE COLOR BROWN

Color the  brown.

BROWN MONKEY

THIS IS THE COLOR BLACK

Color the  black.

BLACK BAT

REVIEWING THE COLORS

Draw lines from the colors to the pictures that are usually those colors, then color the pictures.

REVIEWING THE COLORS

Draw lines from the colors to the pictures that are usually those colors, then color the pictures.

THE COLORS OF THE OCEAN

Color the 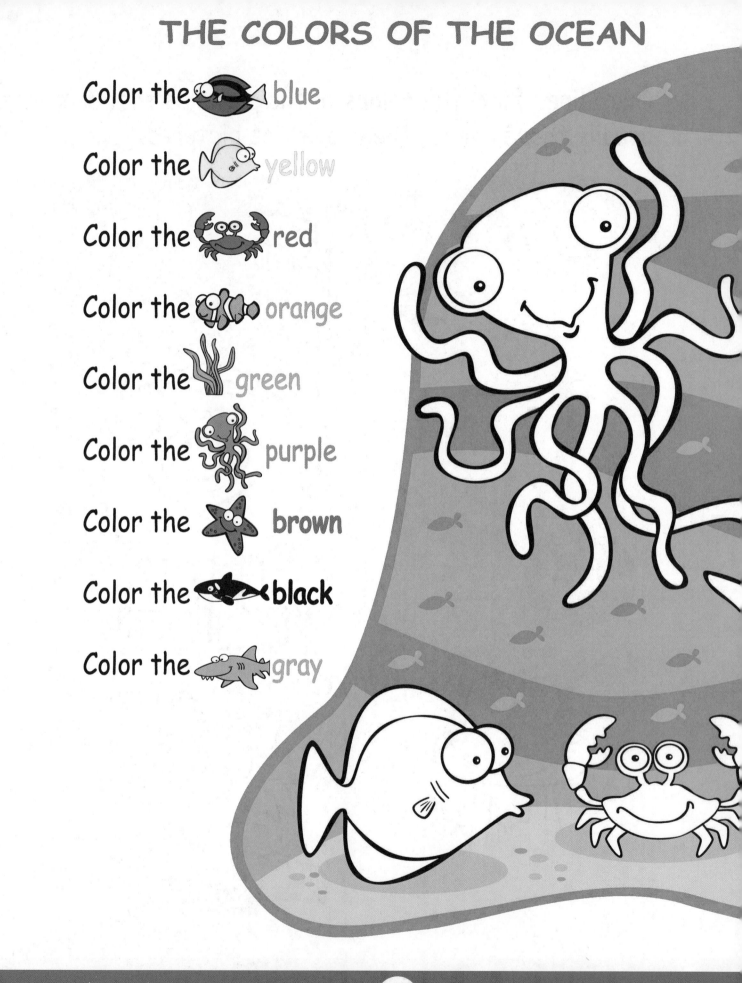 blue

Color the yellow

Color the red

Color the orange

Color the green

Color the purple

Color the brown

Color the black

Color the gray

SHAPES, SHAPES AND MORE SHAPES

Trace the dotted lines to learn the shapes.

square

rectangle

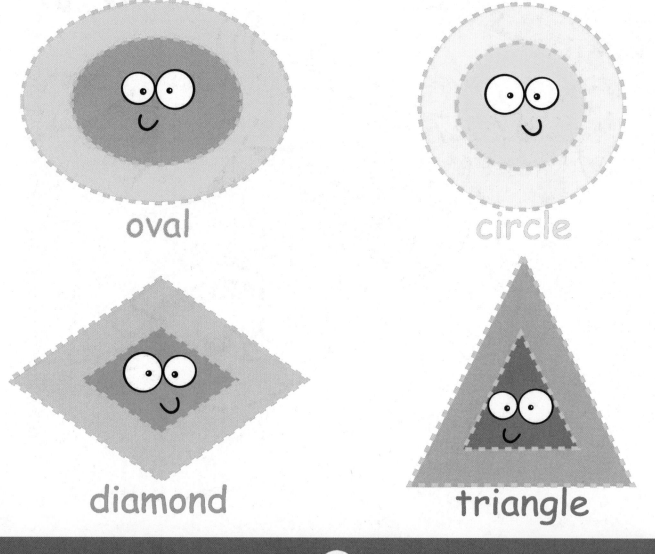

oval

circle

diamond

triangle

ALL KINDS OF SHAPES

Trace the square.

Trace the rectangle.

ALL KINDS OF SHAPES

Trace the oval.

Trace the circle.

ALL KINDS OF SHAPES

Trace the diamond.

Trace the triangle.

DECORATE THE SQUARE CAKES

Trace the squares and then color in the cake.

IT'S TIME FOR SQUARE PRESENTS

Trace the squares and then color in the presents.

Color & Shapes

RECTANGLE DOOR AND WINDOWS

Trace the rectangles, then color in the door and windows.

RECTANGLE DINOSAURS

Trace the rectangles, then color in the dinosaurs.

Colors & Shapes

OVAL PIZZA PIES

Trace the ovals and then add toppings to the pizzas.

OVAL HONEY BEES

Trace the ovals and then color in the bees.

Color & Shapes

DECORATE THE CIRCLE COOKIES

Trace the circles, then color in the cookies.

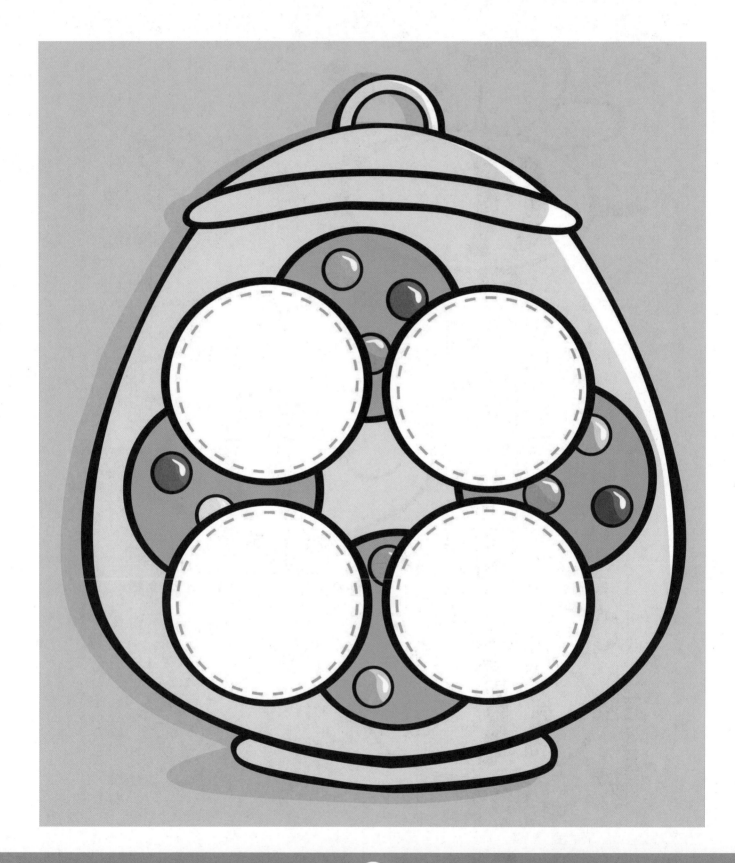

SAY CHEESE CIRCLES

Trace the circles in the cheese and then color them in.

Colors & Shapes

DIAMOND PATTERNED SNAKE

Trace and color the diamonds on the snake.

DIAMOND FISH

Trace the diamonds and then color in the fish.

Color & Shapes

TRIANGLE WINGS

Trace the butterfly's triangle wings then color them in.

WHAT TRIANGLE TEETH YOU HAVE

Trace the triangles, then color in the monster's teeth and spikes.

REVIEWING SHAPES

Trace the circles to finish the picture,
then color the balloons in.

Trace the squares to finish the picture,
then color in the presents.

Trace the triangles to finish the picture,
then color the ice cream cones in.

REVIEWING SHAPES

Trace the rectangles to finish the picture, then color the buildings in.

Trace the ovals to finish the picture, then color in the eggs.

Trace the diamonds to finish the picture, then color the kites in.

BACKYARD SHAPES

Color all the ▢ red.
Color all the ◯ yellow.

PENGUIN SHAPES

Color all the ▽ orange.

Color all the ▭ blue.

DINO OUTDOORS

Color all the ○ purple.
Color all the ◇ green.

ALL KINDS OF SHAPES

Color the picture.

◯ red ▢ orange △ purple

◯ yellow ▭ blue ◇ green

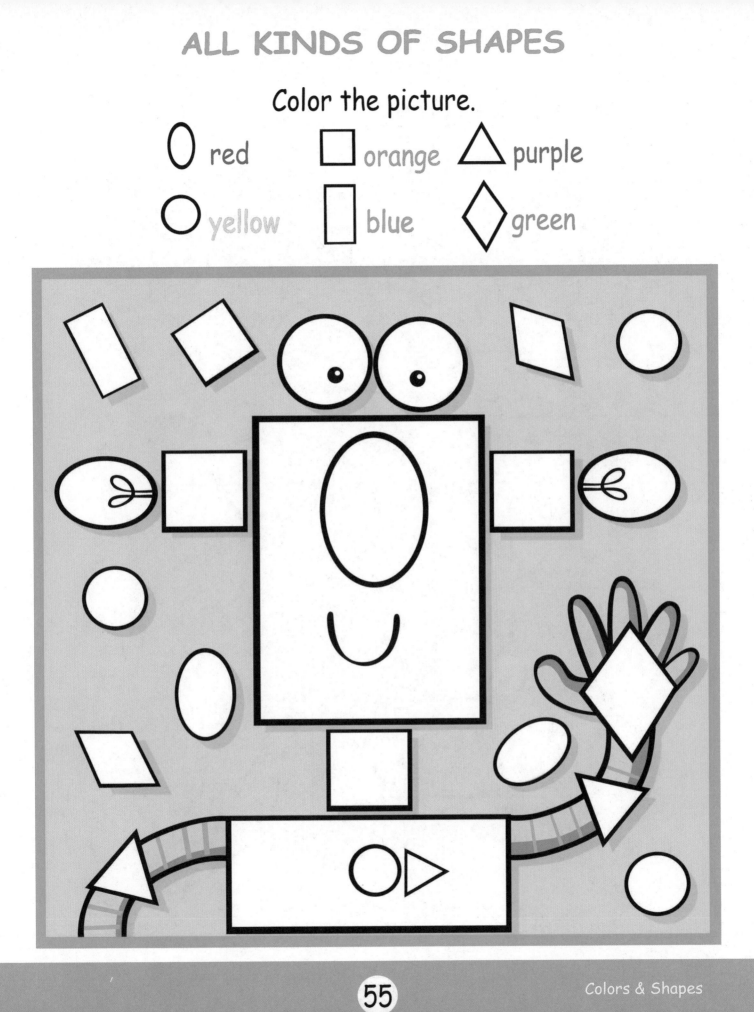

SWIMMING ALONG

Check all the ◯ and ⬭ in this picture.

PARK SHAPES

Check all the ☐ and ☐ in the picture.

SNAKE SHAPES

Color all the △ yellow.

Color all the ◇ orange.

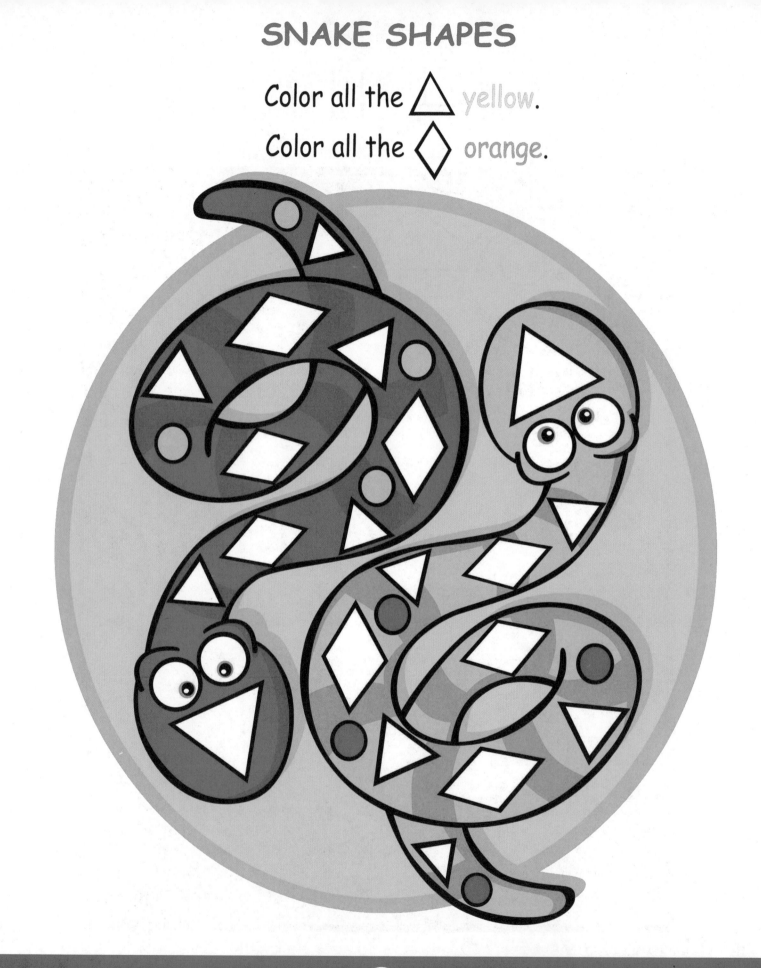

INSECT SHAPES

Check all the ◯ , ⬭ and ▭ in the picture.

SILLY FRUIT SHAPES

Check all the ◯ , △ and ☐ in the picture.

JEWEL SHAPES

Check all the ◯, ◇ and △ in the picture.

PATTERNS

Circle the correct shapes to continue the pattern.

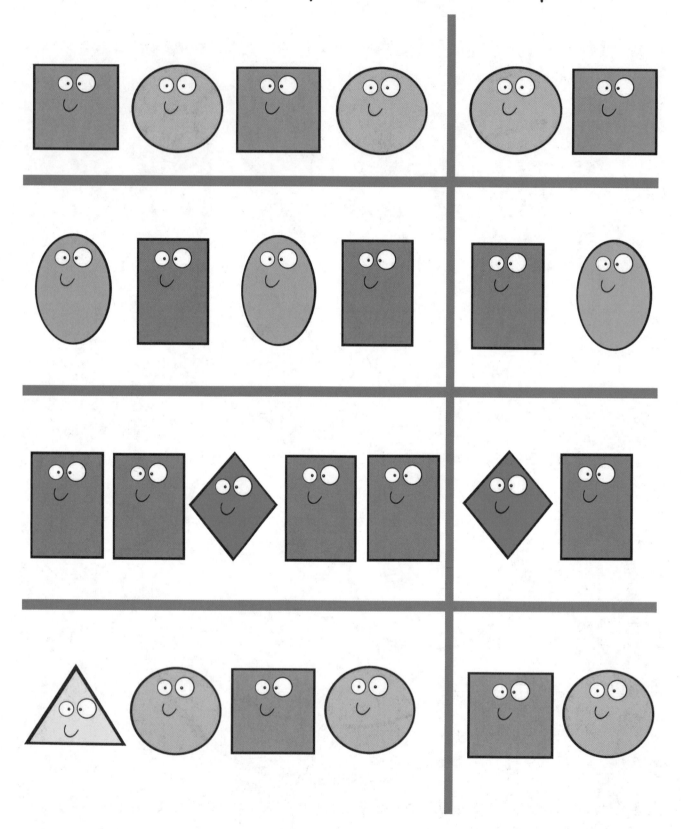

PATTERNS

Circle the correct shapes to continue the pattern.

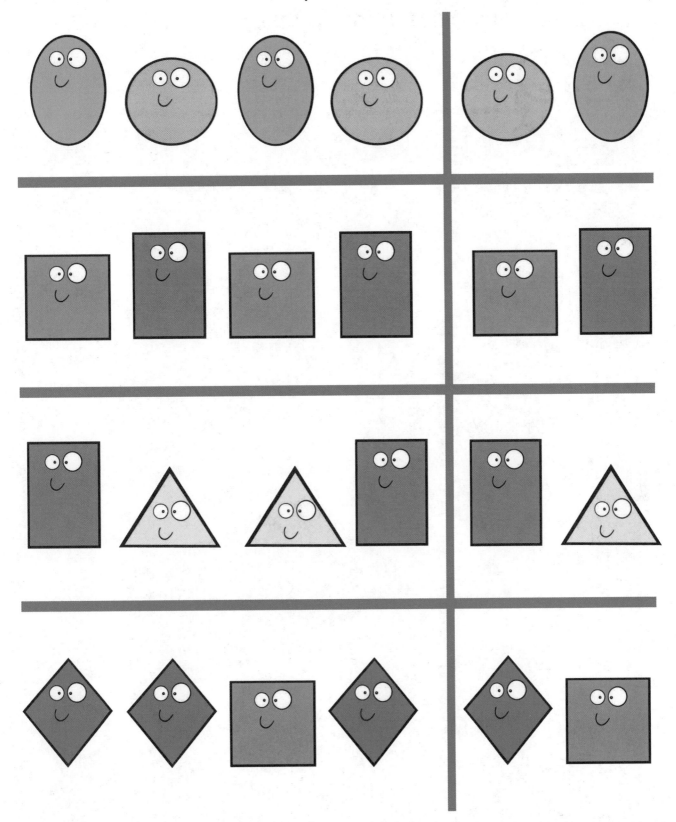

SPIDER FRIENDS

Follow this pattern ■ ▲ ■ ▲ to help the spider get to his friend.

INTO THE WATER

Follow this pattern ▲ ⬤ ▲ ⬤ to help the penguin get to the water and his friend.

RACE TO THE RAINBOW

Follow this pattern  to lead the unicorn to the rainbow.

SHAPE MYSTERY PICTURE
Color the picture.

◯ = yellow ▢ = purple ⬭ = blue △ = green ▭ = orange

TRACING LETTERS A, B, C, D, E & F

Trace the letters with the end of your finger.

TRACING LETTERS G, H, I, J & K

Trace the letters with the end of your finger.

TRACING LETTERS L, M, N, O & P

Trace the letters with the end of your finger.

Trace the letters with the end of your finger.

TRACING LETTERS V, W, X, Y & Z

Trace the letters with the end of your finger.

BEES TO FLOWERS

Draw a line from the uppercase letter to the matching lowercase letter.

A   C   D   B

c   d   a   b

CLOWNING AROUND

Draw a line from the uppercase letter to the matching lowercase letter.

G   F   H   E

SPIDER TO WEB

Draw a line from the uppercase letter to the matching lowercase letter.

I   J   K   L

l   k   j   i

FISHING PENGUINS

Draw a line from the uppercase letter to the matching lowercase letter.

M   N   P   O

o   p   n   m

LADYBUG FLY AWAY HOME

Draw a line from the uppercase letter to the matching lowercase letter.

Q R S T

s q t r

MELTING ICE CREAM

Draw a line from the uppercase letter to the matching lowercase letter.

W   U   V

u   v   w

MAMA TO BABY

Draw a line from the uppercase letter to the matching lowercase letter.

Z   Y   X

x   z   y

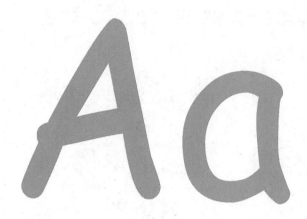

Color the picture.

APPLE

WHAT IS HIDING IN THIS PICTURE?

Color the a's brown.

IT'S AN ACORN

ALLIGATOR & ANT ASTRONAUTS

Circle the 5 hidden A's in the picture.

ANT TO APPLE

Trace a path to help the ant get to the apple.

B b

Color the picture.

BUTTERFLY

WHAT BEGINS WITH THE LETTER B?

Circle the pictures that begin with the letter b.

baseball

fish

spoon

button

bee

cherries

BALLET BEAR

Circle the 5 hidden B's in the picture.

BEE TO HIS HIVE

Trace a path to help the bee get to the hive.

Alphabet

C c

Color the picture.

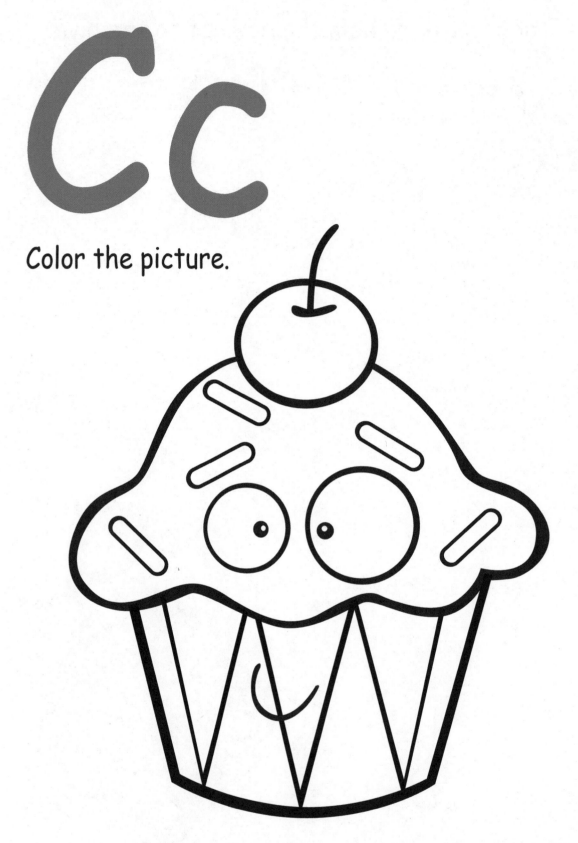

CUPCAKE

FEED THE MONSTER

Draw lines from the pictures that begin with c to the monster's mouth.

cookie

cherries

ice cream cone

cheese

cupcake

banana

AT THE CIRCUS

Circle the 5 hidden C's in the picture.

COW BAKER

Help the cow get to her cupcakes. Trace a path.

Dd

Color the picture.

DEER

WHAT IS HIDING IN THIS PICTURE?

Color all the d's yellow.

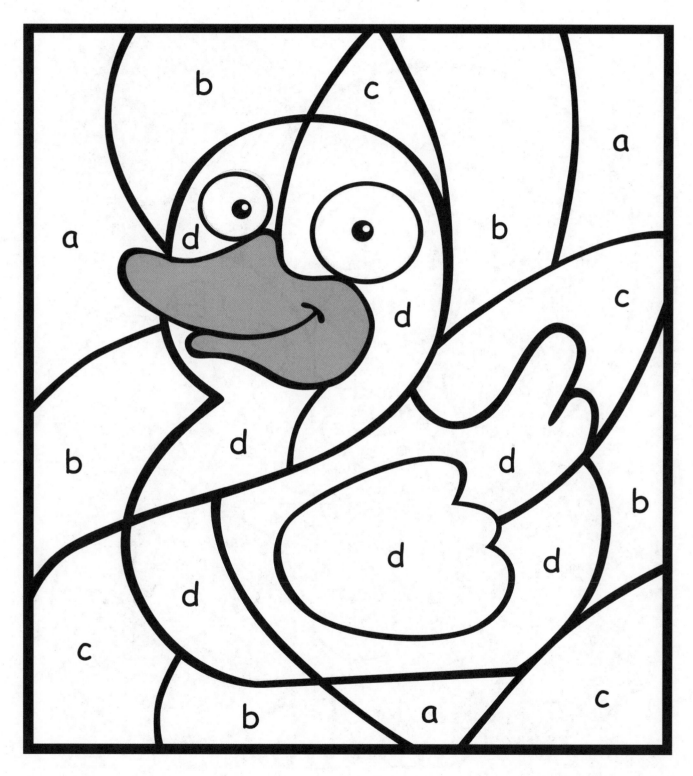

IT'S A DUCK

DONUT EATING DINO

Circle the 5 hidden D's in the picture.

SWIMMING DOLPHIN

Which path will get the dolphin to the top of the ocean? Trace a path with your finger.

Alphabet

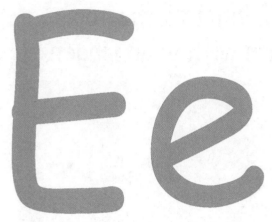

Color the picture.

EARTH

E IS FOR ELEPHANT

Color the elephants that have the letter e on them.

A RIDE UP HIGH

Circle the 5 hidden E's in the picture.

EAGLE'S NEST

Trace a path to help the eagle get to her eggs.

Alphabet

REVIEWING A, B, C, D & E

Trace the path from the picture to the letter that belongs to its name.

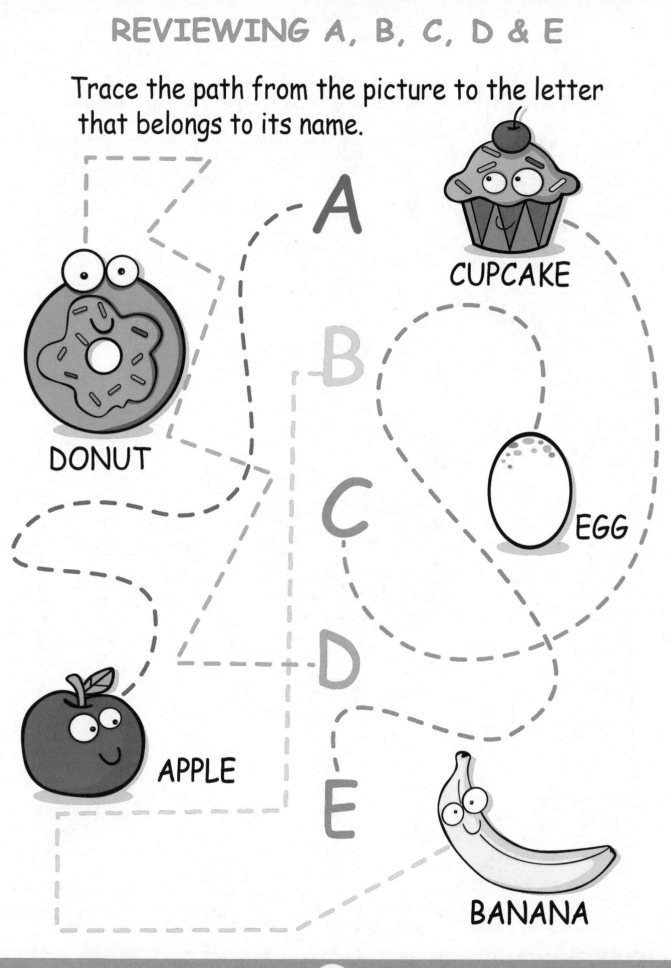

CUPCAKE

A

DONUT

B

C

EGG

D

APPLE

E

BANANA

Trace the path from the picture to the letter that belongs to its name.

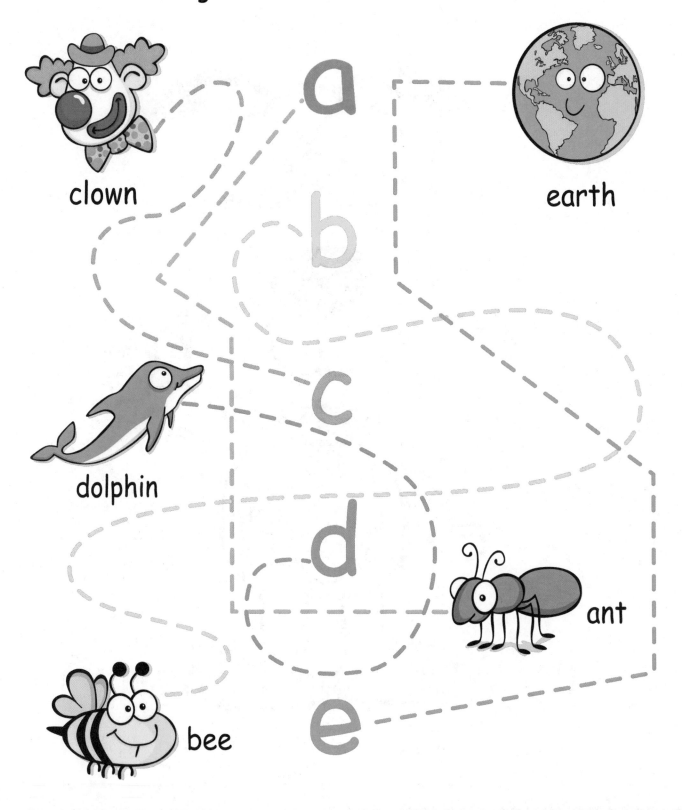

clown

earth

dolphin

ant

bee

a

b

c

d

e

REVIEWING LETTERS A,B,C,D & E.

Connect the dots from A to E, then color in the picure.

REVIEWING A, B, C, D & E

Trace the uppercase letters.

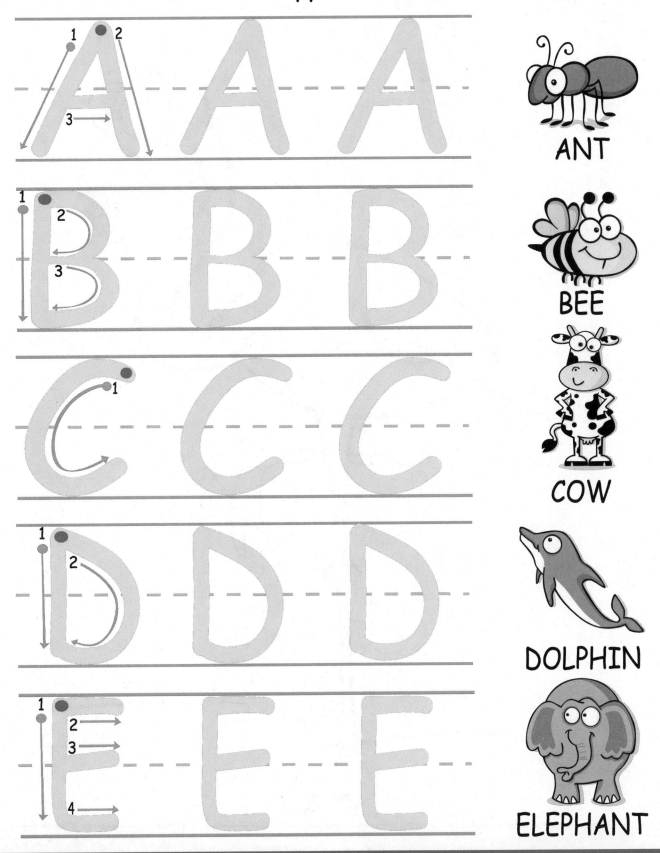

ANT

BEE

COW

DOLPHIN

ELEPHANT

Alphabet

F f

Color the picture.

FLAMINGO

F IS FOR FISH

Color the fish that have the letter f on them.

MAKE A WISH

Circle the 5 hidden F's in the picture.

MAMA FROG IS ON HER WAY

Which path will take the frog to her baby tadpoles?
Trace a path with your finger.

Gg

Color the picture.

WHAT IS HIDING IN THIS PICTURE?

Color the g's orange.

IT'S A GOLDFISH

GINGERBREAD ROCK

Circle the 5 hidden G's in the picture.

GRAPE-GOBBLING GOAT

Trace a path to help the goat get a nibble of the grapes.

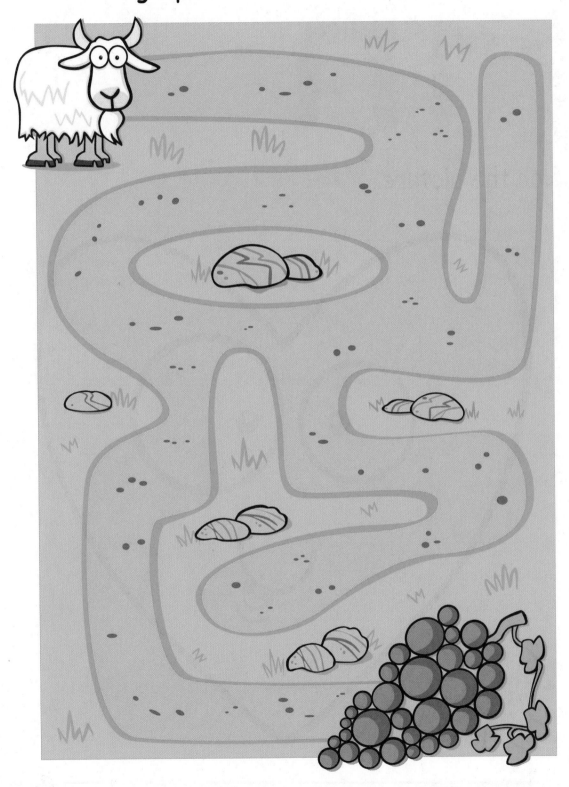

Color the picture.

HEART

WHAT BEGINS WITH THE LETTER H?

Circle the pictures that begin with the letter h.

moon

house

hot dog

scissors

snowman

hippo

LUNCH TIME

Circle the 5 hidden H's in the picture.

FROM FIELD TO BARN

Trace a path to help the horse from the field to the barn.

Ii

Color the picture.

WHAT IS HIDING IN THIS PICTURE?

Color the i's green.

IT'S AN IGUANA

IGUANA ENJOYING ICE CREAM

Circle the 5 hidden I's in the picture.

ICE SKATING IGUANA

Which path will take the iguana to the tasty mug of hot chocolate? Trace a path with your finger.

J j

Color the picture.

JELLYFISH

WHAT BEGINS WITH THE LETTER J?

Circle the pictures that begin with the letter j.

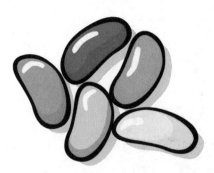

jellybeans

pencil

key

jacks

jug

tooth

JELLY BEAN JAR

Circle the 5 hidden J's in the picture.

A SNACK OF BREAD AND JAM

Which of the jellyfish's tentacles lead to the jar of strawberry jam? Trace a path with your finger.

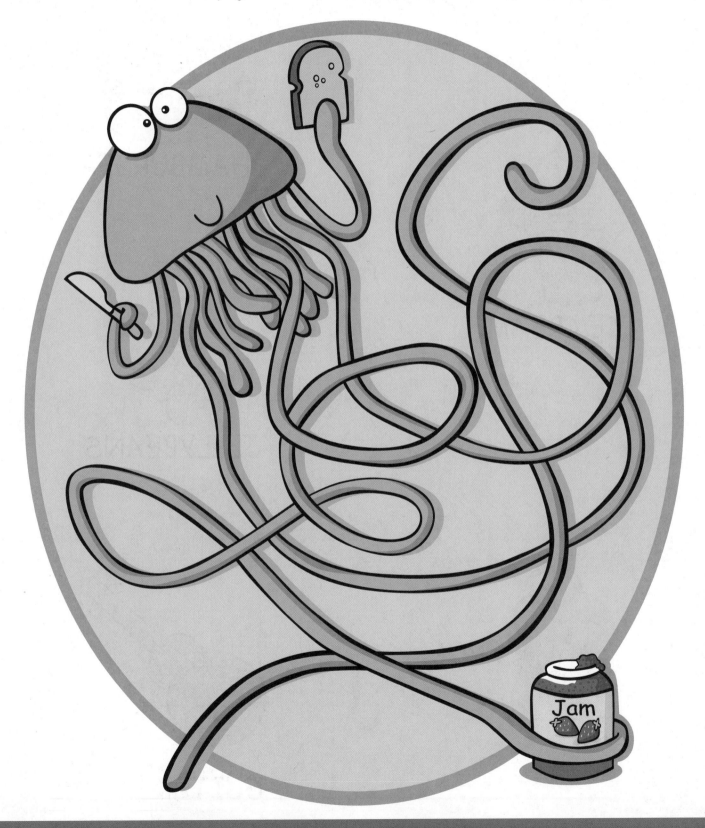

Alphabet

REVIEWING F, G, H, I & J

Trace the path from the picture to the letter that belongs to its name.

F

HAMBURGER

ICE CREAM

G

JELLYBEANS

H

I

FROG

J

GUITAR

REVIEWING F, G, H, I & J

Trace the path from the picture to the letter that belongs to its name.

house

jam

f

g

fish

h

giraffe

i

igloo

j

REVIEWING LETTERS F,G,H,I & J

Connect the dots from A to J, then color in the picture.

REVIEWING F, G, H, I & J

Trace the uppercase letters.

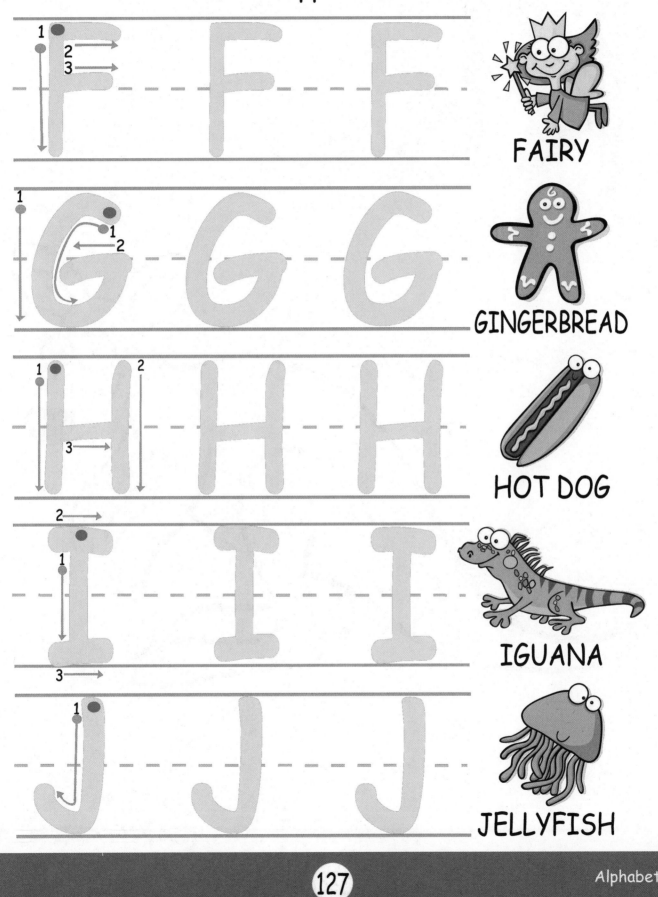

FAIRY

GINGERBREAD

HOT DOG

IGUANA

JELLYFISH

Color the picture.

KANGAROO

K IS FOR KEYS

Color the keys that have the letter k on them.

A KING AND HIS KNIGHT

Circle the 5 hidden K's in the picture.

LET'S GO FLY A KITE

Which kite string is the baby kangaroo holding?
Trace a path with your finger.

Ll

Color the picture.

LION

WHAT BEGINS WITH THE LETTER L?

Circle the pictures that begin with the letter l.

ladybug

snail

watermelon

lemon

cheese

lamp

SHARING A LEMON LOLLIPOP

Circle the 5 hidden L's in the picture.

LADYBUG COME HOME

Trace a path to help the ladybug get home to her leaf.

Mm

Color the picture.

MUSHROOM

WHAT IS HIDING IN THIS PICTURE?

Color the m's gray.

IT'S A MOUSE

MONSTERS ON THE MOON

Circle the 5 hidden M's in the picture.

MOUSE HOUSE

Help the mouse find his way to his mushroom house. Trace a path.

Nn

Color the picture.

NARWHAL

WHAT BEGINS WITH THE LETTER N?

Circle the pictures that begin with the letter n.

needle

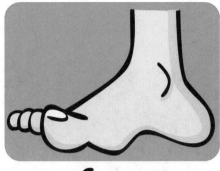

foot

acorn

nose

numbers

toaster

FEEDING TIME

Circle the 5 hidden N's in the picture.

NOODLE-EATING NEWT

Which noodle leads to the newt's mouth?
Trace a path with your finger.

Oo

Color the picture.

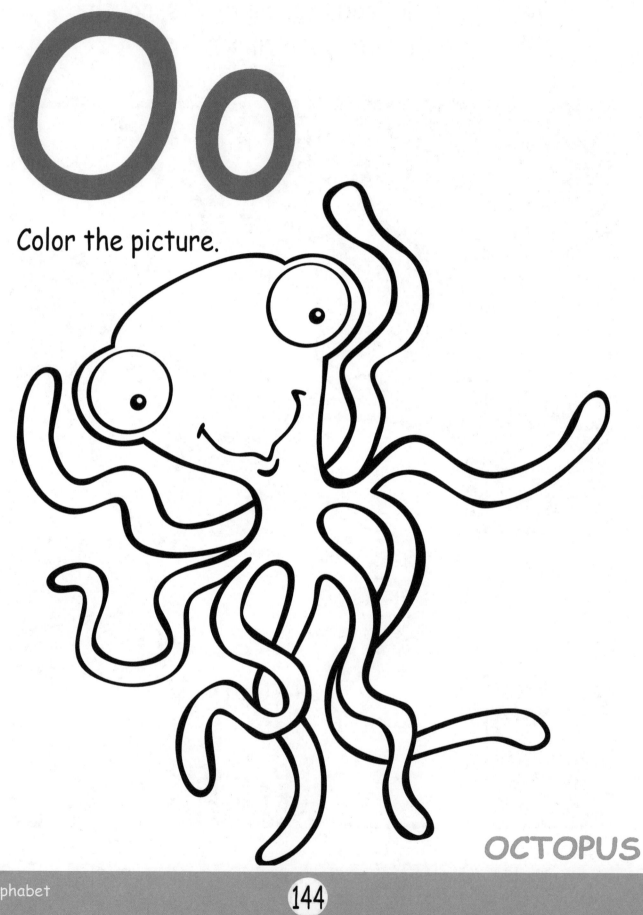

OCTOPUS

O IS FOR OWL

Color the owls that have the letter o on them.

TIME TO BAKE ORANGE MUFFINS

Circle the 5 hidden O's in the picture.

OCTOPUS CAVE IN THE OCEAN

Help the octopus get home to her mother.
Trace a path.

Alphabet

REVIEWING K, L, M, N & O

Trace the path from the picture to the letter that belongs to its name.

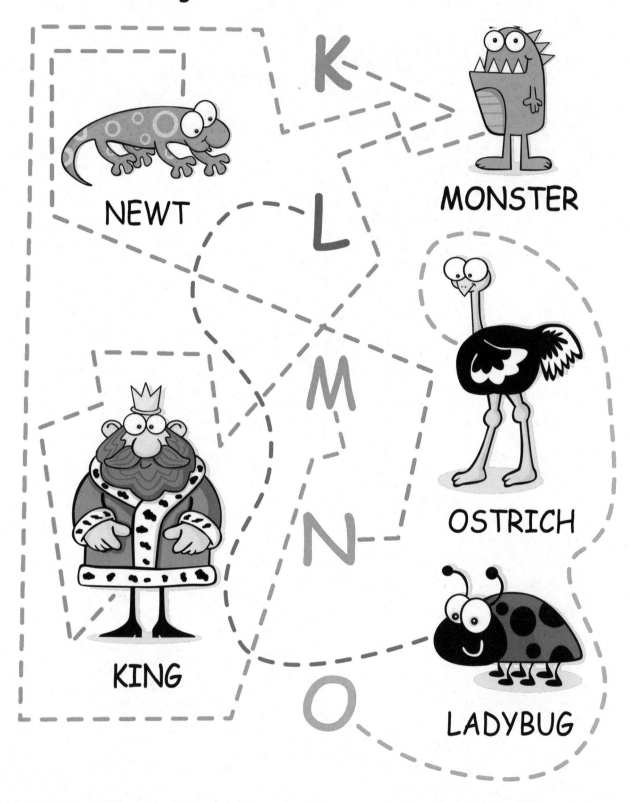

NEWT

MONSTER

K

L

M

N

O

OSTRICH

KING

LADYBUG

REVIEWING K, L, M, N & O

Trace the path from the picture to the letter that belongs to its name.

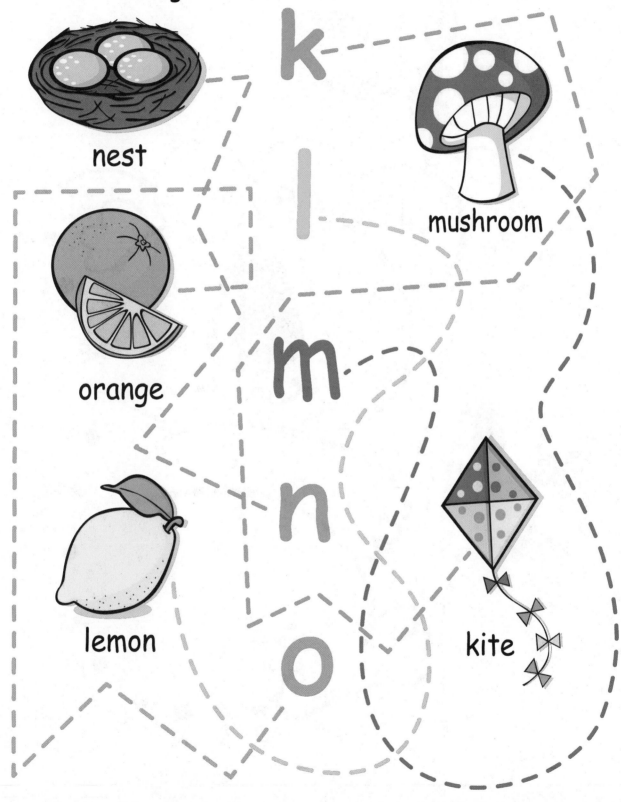

nest

k

mushroom

l

orange

m

lemon

n

o

kite

REVIEWING LETTERS K, L, M, N & O

Connect the dots from A to O, then color in the picture.

REVIEWING K, L, M, N & O

Trace the uppercase letters.

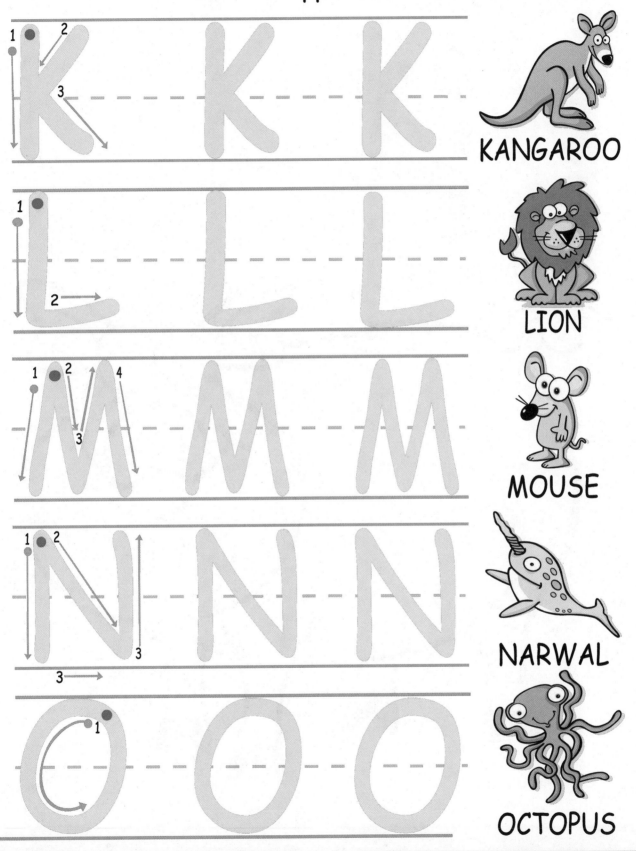

KANGAROO

LION

MOUSE

NARWAL

OCTOPUS

P p

Color the picture.

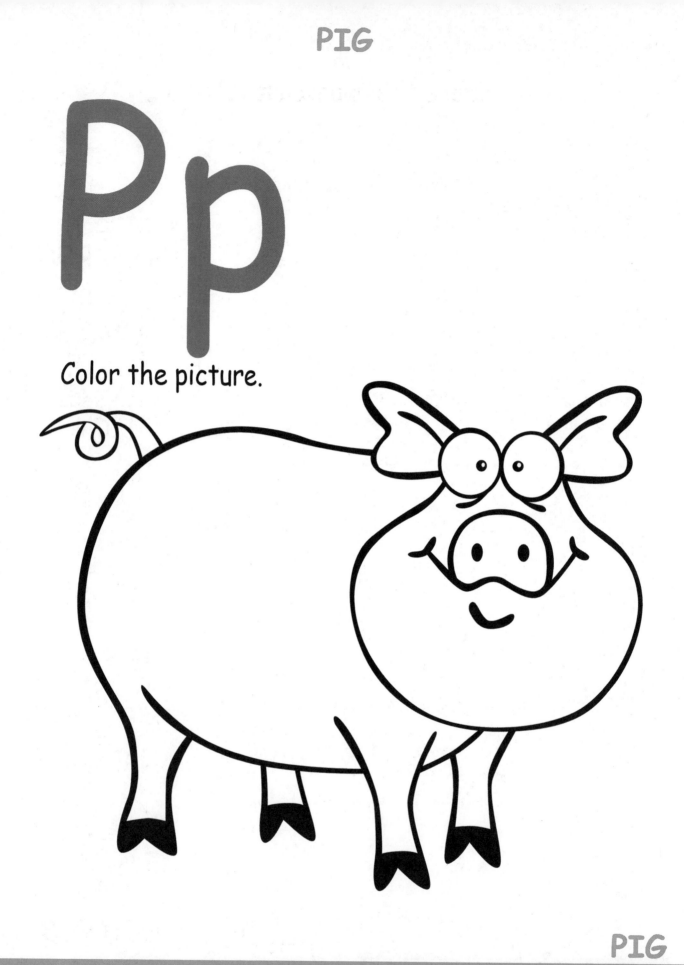

WHAT BEGINS WITH THE LETTER P?

Circle the pictures that begin with the letter p.

pencil

shark

mouse

pizza

penguin

flamingo

POLAR BEAR PIZZA MAKER

Circle the 5 hidden P's in the picture.

PIGLETS TO PARENTS

Help the piglets get to their parents in the center of the pig pen. Trace a path.

Alphabet

Qq

Color the picture.

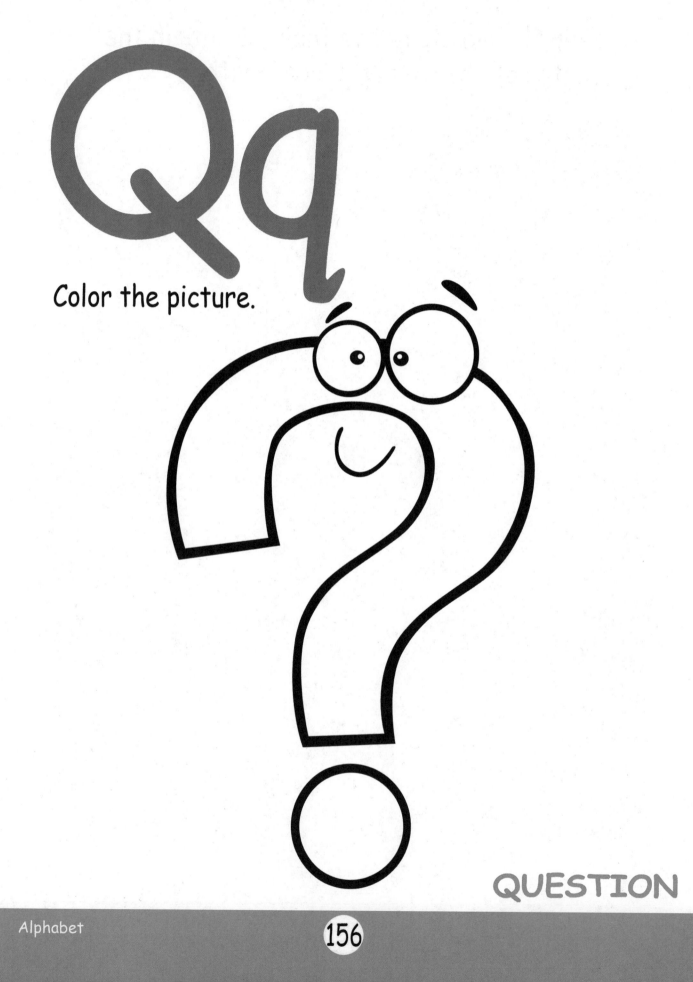

WHAT IS HIDING IN THIS PICTURE?

Color the q's blue.

IT'S A QUAIL

QUILTING QUEEN

Circle the 5 hidden Q's in the picture.

QUILL TO PAPER

Which ink line goes from the quill to the letter the queen has signed? Trace a path with your finger.

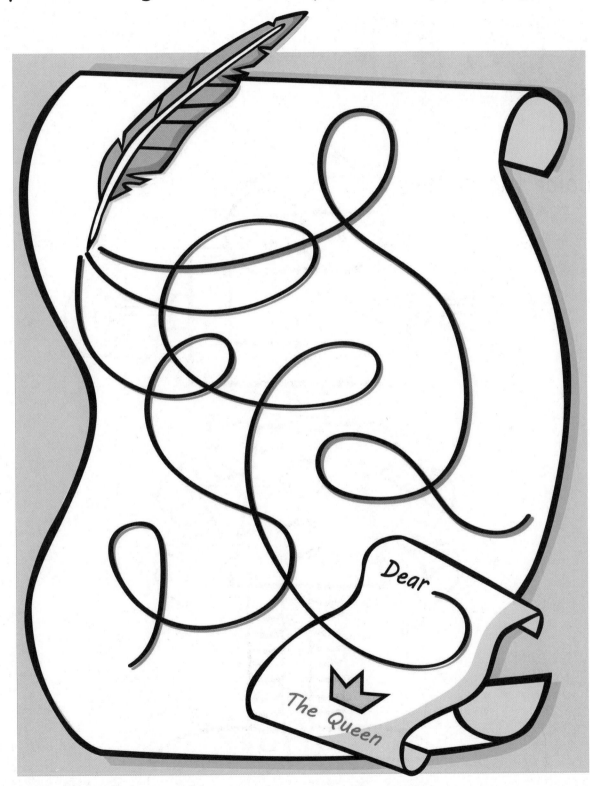

Alphabet

Rr

Color the picture.

ROBOT

WHAT BEGINS WITH THE LETTER R?

Circle the pictures that begin with the letter r.

cookie

rainbow

rhinoceros

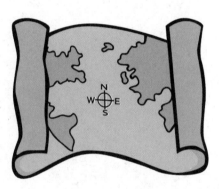

map

football

rocketship

RABBIT, ROBOT & ROCKETSHIPS

Circle the 5 hidden R's in the picture.

ROBOT IN THE RAIN

Help the robot get home and out of the rain before he gets rusty. Trace a path.

Ss

Color the picture.

SNAKE

WHAT IS HIDING IN THIS PICTURE?

Color the s's pink.

IT'S A SEAHORSE

SQUIRREL ON A SUNNY DAY

Circle the 5 hidden S's in the picture.

SHARK SMELLS HIS DINNER

Can you lead the shark to his dinner?
Trace a path.

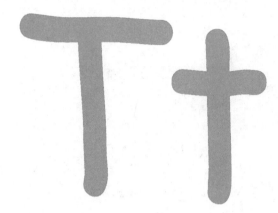

Color the picture.

TURTLE

T IS FOR TEETH

Circle the teeth that have the letter t on them.

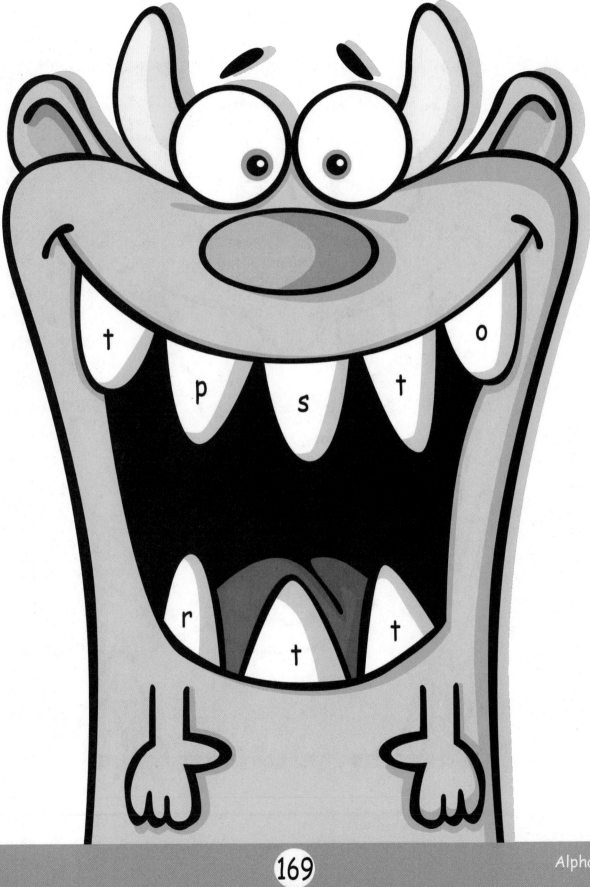

Alphabet

SMILING TURTLE

Circle the 5 hidden T's in the picture.

THE TOOTH FAIRY

Trace a path to help the tooth find its way under the pillow.

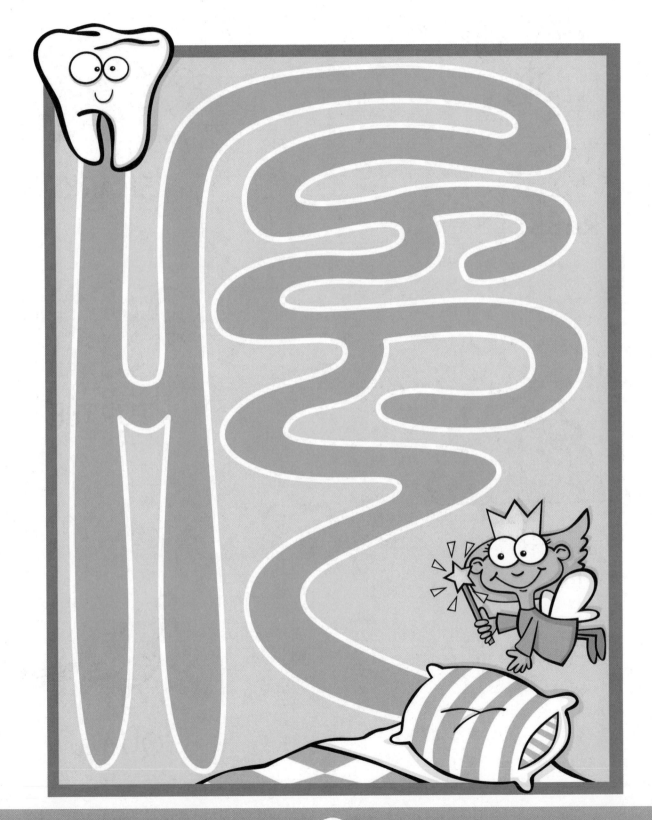

Alphabet

REVIEWING P, Q, R, S & T

Trace the path from the picture to the letter that belongs to its name.

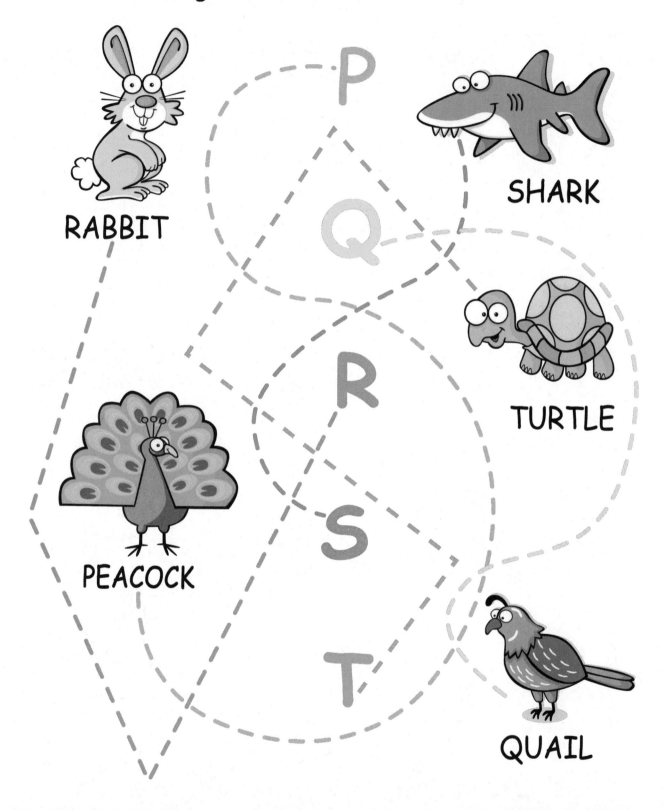

RABBIT

SHARK

P

Q

TURTLE

R

PEACOCK

S

T

QUAIL

REVIEWING P, Q, R, S & T

Trace the path from the picture to the letter that belongs to its name.

strawberry

tea pot

raspberry

pineapple

question

p

q

r

s

t

REVIEWING LETTERS P, Q, R, S & T

Connect the dots from A to T, then color in the picture.

REVIEWING P, Q, R, S & T

Trace the uppercase letters.

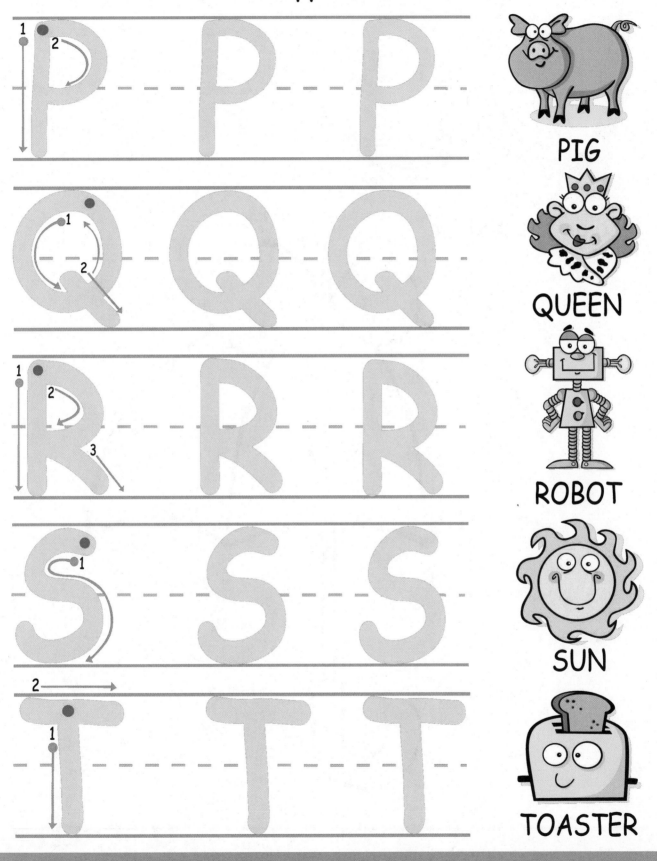

PIG

QUEEN

ROBOT

SUN

TOASTER

Uu

Color the picture.

UMBRELLA

U IS FOR UNICORN

Color the unicorns that have the letter u on them.

UNICORN RIDING A UNICYCLE

Circle the 5 hidden U's in the picture.

RAINDROPS

Trace with your finger the path of the raindrops to see which one is landing on the umbrella.

Alphabet

Vv

Color the picture.

VASE

WHAT BEGINS WITH THE LETTER V?

Circle the pictures that begin with the letter v.

vest

apple

goat

violin

volcano

puffin

VIOLET VIOLIN

Circle the 5 hidden V's in the picture.

WATERING THE VEGGIE PATCH

Lead Farmer Carrot to the patch so it can be watered. Trace a path.

W w

Color the picture.

WHALE

WHAT IS HIDING IN THIS PICTURE?

Color the w's green.

IT'S A WORM

SHIPWRECK

Circle the 5 hidden W's in the picture.

WORM'S HOME

Help Worm get back to his home.
Trace a path.

Color the picture.

XYLOPHONE

WHAT BEGINS OR ENDS WITH THE LETTER X?

Circle the pictures that begin or end with the letter x.

fish

fox

x-ray

banana

balloon

xylophone

X-RAY OF FOX ON BOX

Circle the 5 hidden X's in the picture.

XYLOPHONE

Help the mallets find their way back to the xylophone so the concert can begin.
Trace a path.

Alphabet

Yy

Color the picture.

YARN

WHAT BEGINS WITH THE LETTER Y?

Circle the pictures that begin with the letter y.

yolk

car

balloon

yo-yo

yak

clown

YAK YOGA

Circle the 5 hidden Y's in the picture.

YAK YO-YO

Which string leads from the yo-yo to the yak?
Trace a path with your finger.

Zz

Color the picture.

WHAT BEGINS WITH THE LETTER Z?

Circle the pictures that begin with the letter z.

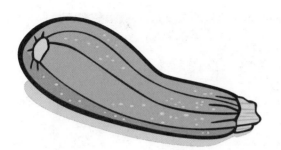

zucchini

watermelon

ant

zebra

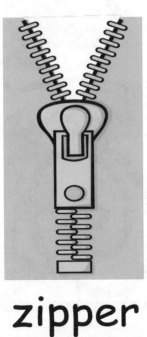

zipper

frog

ZEBRAS AT THE ZOO

Circle the 5 hidden Z's in the picture.

HUNGRY ZEBRA

Help the zebra zig zag through the maze so he can munch on some zucchini. Trace a path.

FREE
zucchini

REVIEWING U, V, W, X, Y & Z

Trace the path from the picture to the letter that belongs to its name.

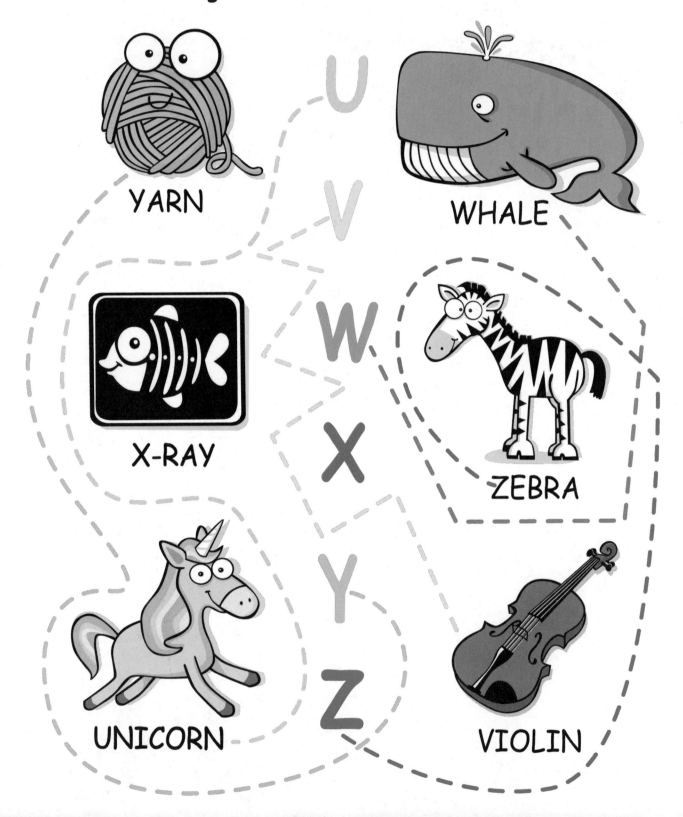

YARN

WHALE

U

V

X-RAY

W

ZEBRA

X

UNICORN

Y

VIOLIN

Z

REVIEWING U, V, W, X, Y & Z

Trace the path from the picture to the letter that belongs to its name.

yak

x-ray

U

V

W

unicycle

zipper

X

Y

watermelon

Z

vulture

REVIEWING LETTERS U,V,W,X,Y & Z

Connect the dots from A to Z, then color in the picture.

ABCDEFGHIJKLMNOPQRSTUVWXYZ

REVIEWING U, V, W, X, Y & Z

Trace the uppercase letters.

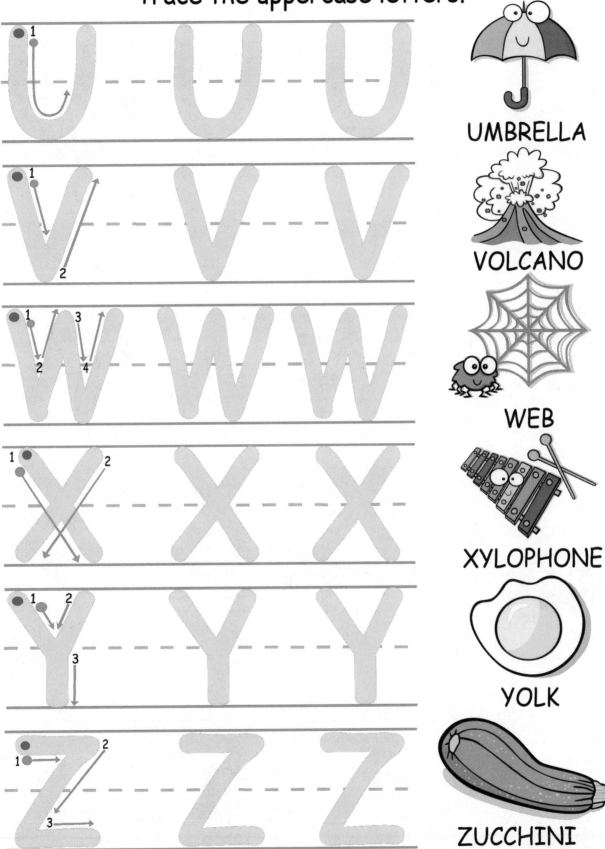

UMBRELLA

VOLCANO

WEB

XYLOPHONE

YOLK

ZUCCHINI

ALPHABETICALLY

Trace the letters.

Alphabet

A TASTY GINGERBREAD HOUSE

Connect the dots from a to z, then color in the picture.

abcdefghijklmnopqrstuvwxyz

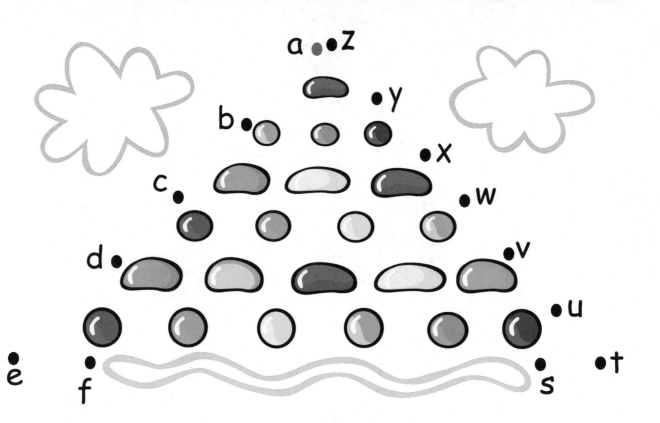
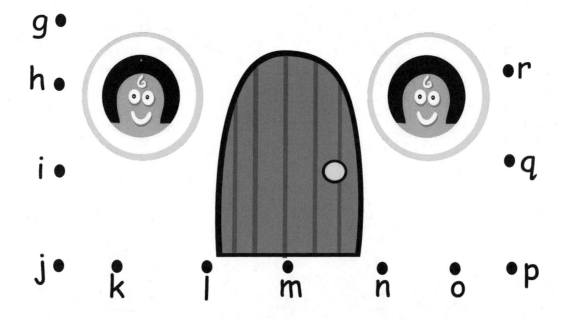

ALPHABET MEMORY

Look at the letters and try to remember them.
Then turn to page 208.

ALPHABET MEMORY

Circle the letters you remember from page 207.

SLITHERING IN THE GRASS

Connect the dots from a to z, then color in the picture.

abcdefghijklmnopqrstuvwxyz

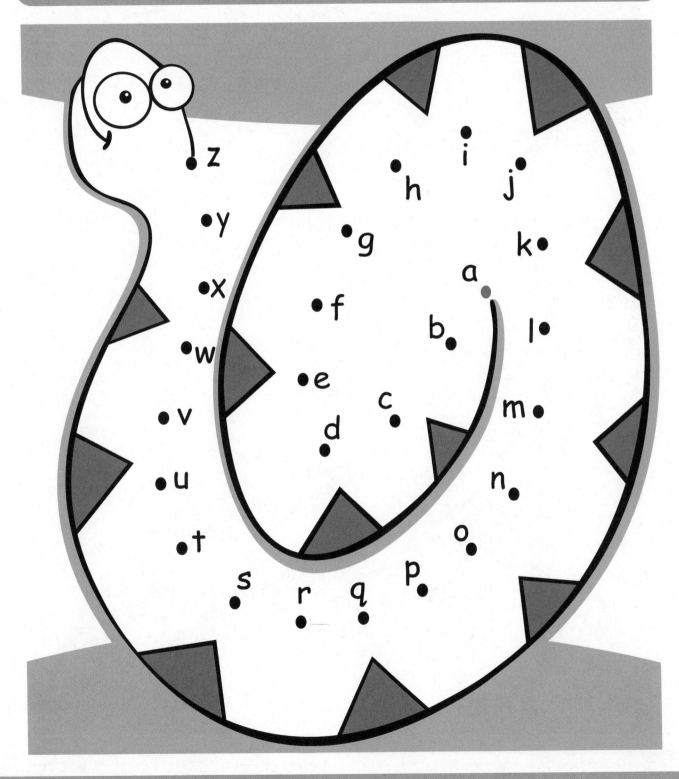

OVER THE RAINBOW

Trace a path from A to Z.

ABCDEFGHIJKLMNOPQRSTUVWXYZ

BOTTOM OF THE OCEAN

Trace a path from a to z.

abcdefghijklmnopqrstuvwxyz

Alphabet

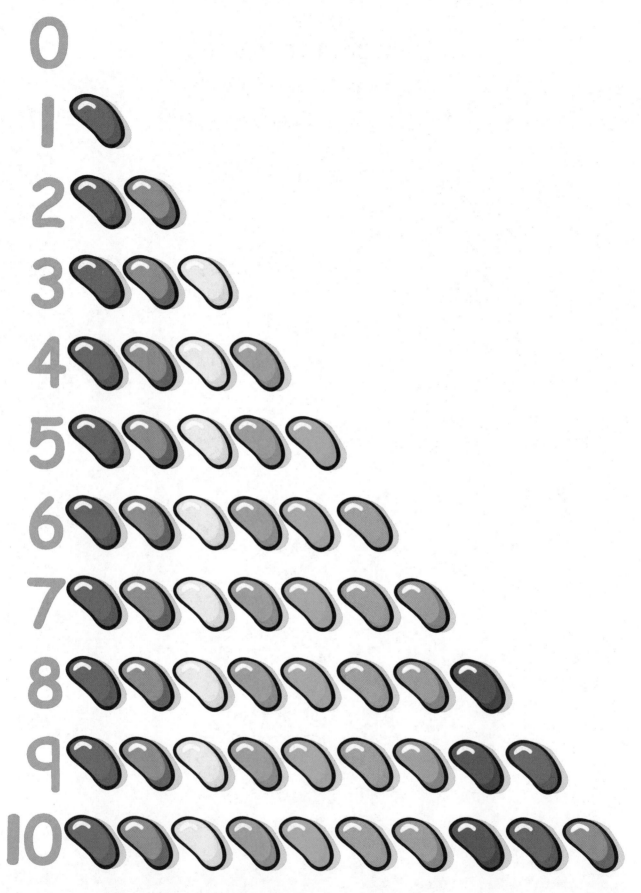

NUMBERS 0-10

Trace the numbers.

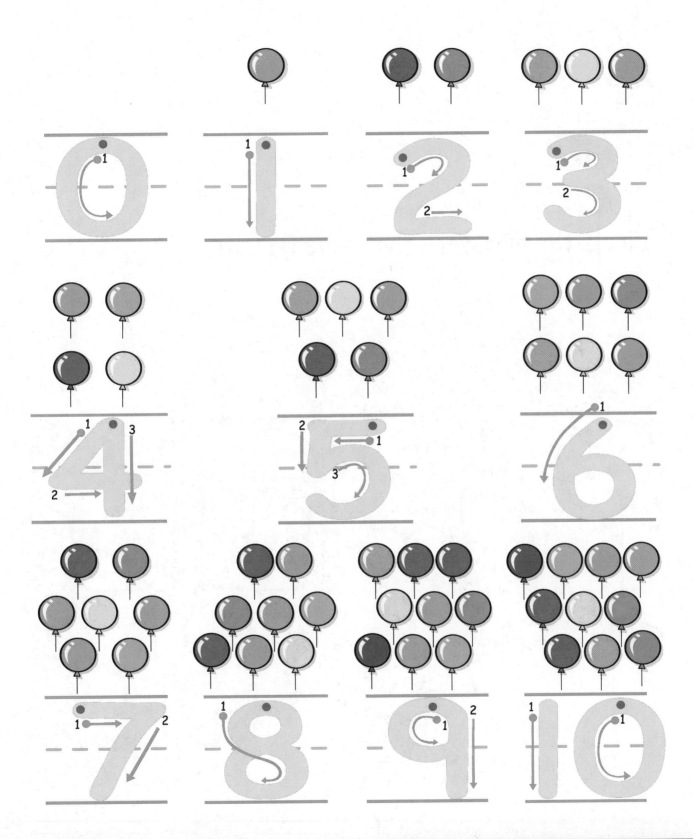

0
zero

Circle the monsters that have 0 spots.

Color the fish that have 0 stripes.

I

one

Circle the bees that are carrying 1 flower.

Circle the insects that are in a group of 1.

2

two

Trace along the dotted line to add 2 oranges to the picnic basket. Then color them in.

Draw lines from the number 2 to the groups of 2.

2

three

Circle the frogs that have 3 spots.

Circle the groups of 3 tadpoles.

4

four

Circle the groups of 4 penguins.

Trace with your finger the path the penguin will take to get to the number 4.

THE NUMBER FIVE

5
five

Circle the clowns that have 5 spots on their pants, then finish coloring the clowns in.

Draw lines from the number 5 to the groups of 5.

REVIEWING NUMBERS 0, 1, 2, 3, 4 & 5

Draw a line from the number to the same number of monsters.

0

1

2

3

4

5

REVIEWING NUMBERS 0, 1, 2, 3, 4 & 5

Trace the numbers.

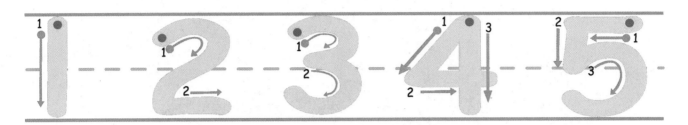

Count the penguins, then circle the correct number.

0 1 2 3 4 5

0 1 2 3 4 5

0 1 2 3 4 5

0 1 2 3 4 5

0 1 2 3 4 5

0 1 2 3 4 5

FINDING 1

Circle the image that you see 1 of in the picture below.

FINDING 2

Circle the image that you see
2 of in the picture below.

Numbers 0-10

FINDING 3

Circle the image that you see
3 of in the picture below.

FINDING 4

Circle the image that you see
4 of in the picture below.

Numbers 0-10

FINDING 5

Circle the image that you see
5 of in the picture below.

HERE COMES THE SUN

Connect the dots from 1 to 5, then color in the picture.

| 1 | 2 | 3 | 4 | 5 |

Numbers 0-10

IT'S RAINING

Connect the dots from 1 to 5, then color in the picture.

1 2 3 4 5

LET IT SNOW

Connect the dots from 1 to 5, then color in the picture.

1 2 3 4 5

HAPPY BIRTHDAY!

Connect the dots from 1 to 5, then color in the picture.

| 1 | 2 | 3 | 4 | 5 |

UP, UP AND AWAY

Connect the dots from 1 to 5, then color in the picure.

Numbers 0-10

THE NUMBER SIX

6

six

Circle the groups of 6 ants.

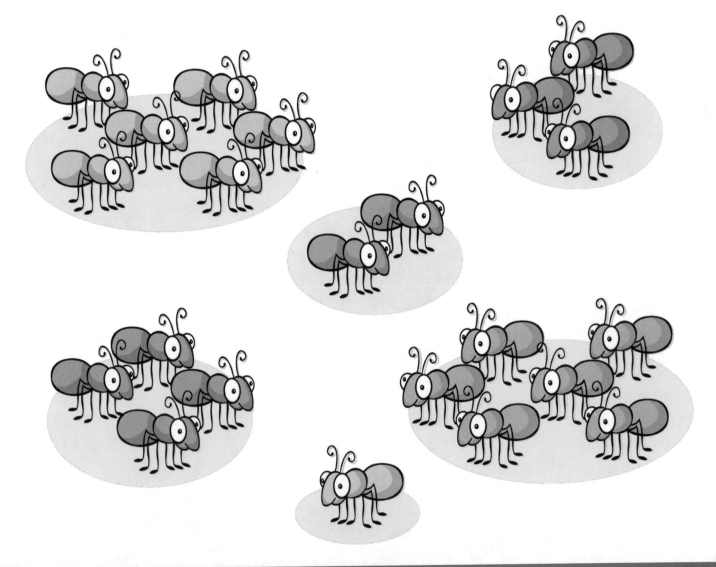

Lead the ants to their home in the ground marked with the number 6. Trace a path.

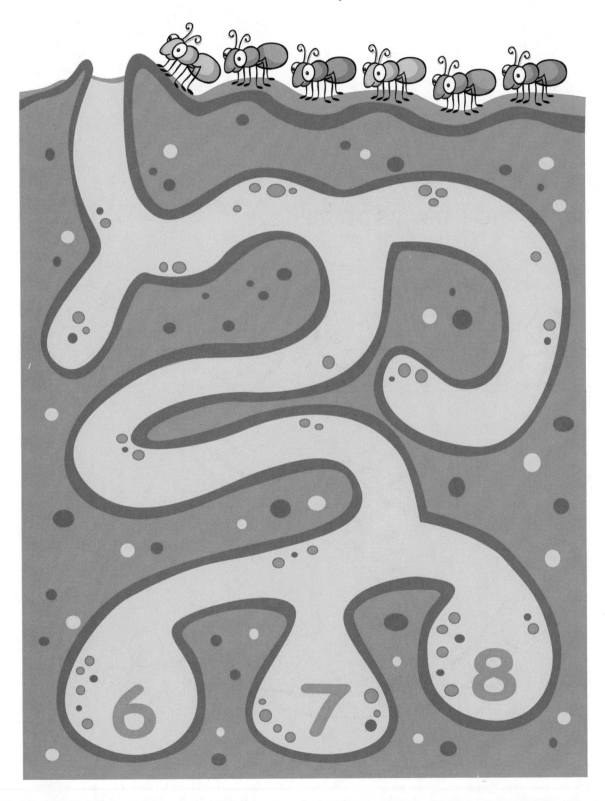

7

seven

Color in the 7 pieces of fruit.

Circle the groups of 7 pieces of fruit.

8

eight

Trace the dotted lines to finish the 8 tentacles on the octopus. Then color in the picture.

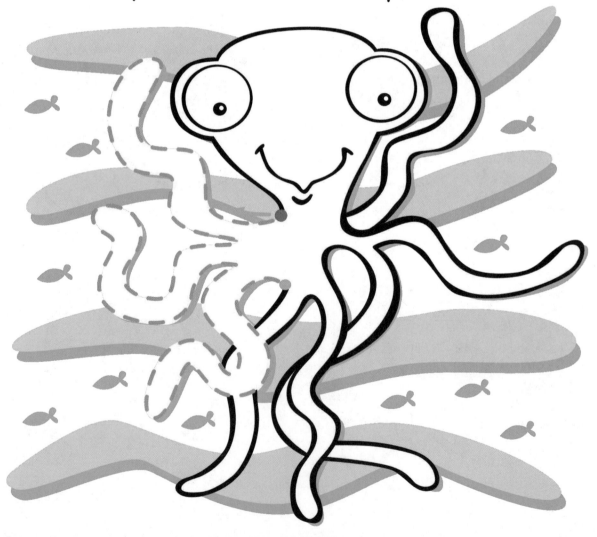

Circle the groups of 8 sea creatures.

9
nine

Circle the cookies that have 9 spots on them.

Draw lines from the number 9 to the groups of 9.

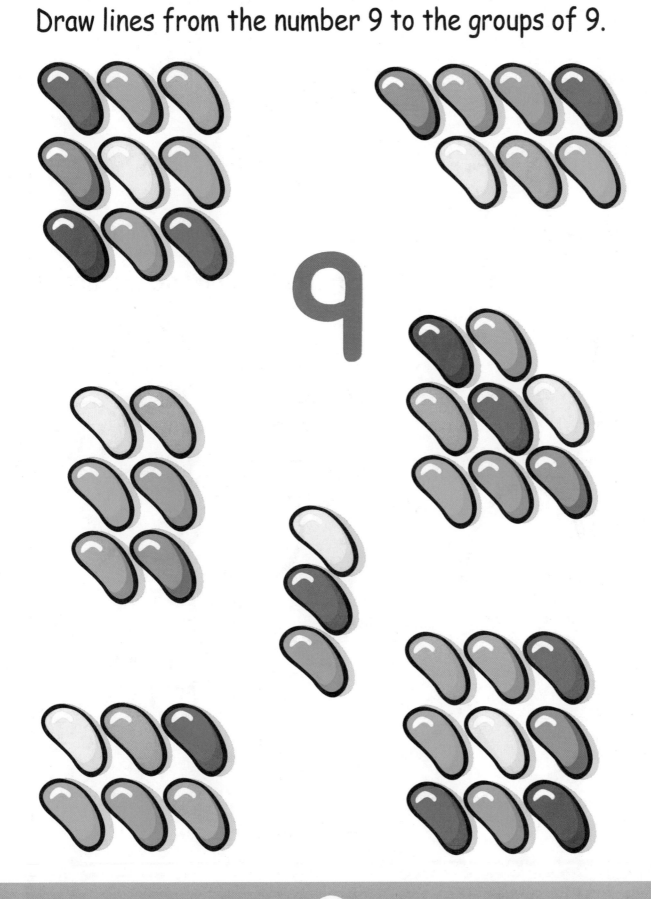

10

ten

Draw 10 spots on the fish, then color the picture in.

Draw lines from the number 10 to the groups of 10 fish.

REVIEWING NUMBERS 6, 7, 8, 9 & 10

Draw a line from the number to the same number of bugs.

6

7

8

9

10

REVIEWING NUMBERS 6, 7, 8, 9 & 10

Trace the numbers.

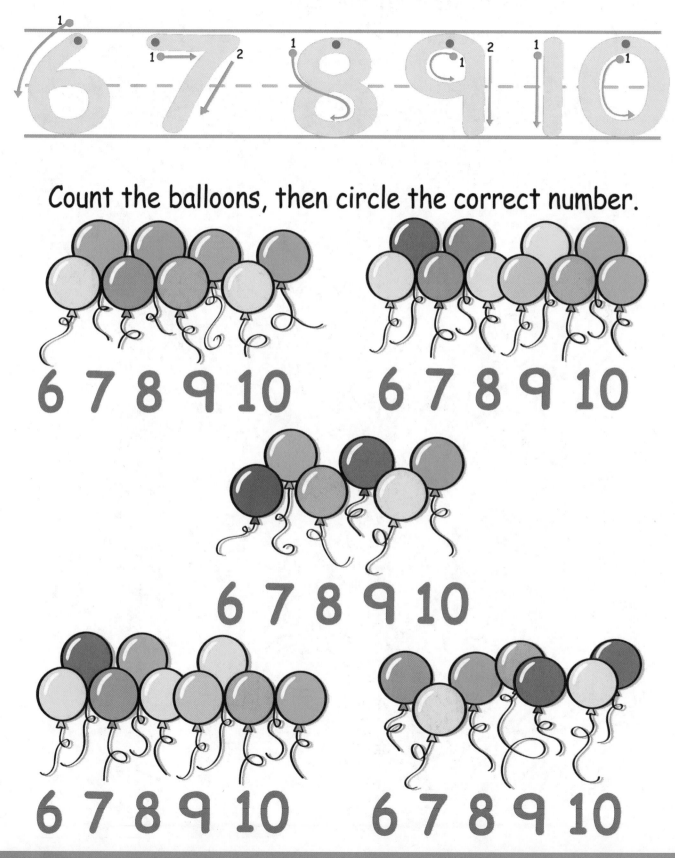

Count the balloons, then circle the correct number.

6 7 8 9 10   6 7 8 9 10

6 7 8 9 10

6 7 8 9 10   6 7 8 9 10

FINDING 6

Circle the image that you see 6 of in the picture below.

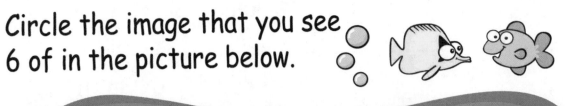

FINDING 7

Circle the image that you see
7 of in the picture below.

FINDING 8

Circle the image that you see
8 of in the picture below.

FINDING 9

Circle the image that you see
9 of in the picture below.

FINDING 10

Circle the image that you see 10 of in the picture below.

FISHY FUN

Connect the dots from 1 to 10, then color in the picture.

| 1 | 2 | 3 | 4 | 5 | 6 | 7 | 8 | 9 | 10 |

BUZZING ALONG

Connect the dots from 1 to 10, then color in the picture.

1 2 3 4 5 6 7 8 9 10

JUST SWIMMING ALONG

Connect the dots from 1 to 10, then color in the picture.

| 1 | 2 | 3 | 4 | 5 | 6 | 7 | 8 | 9 | 10 |

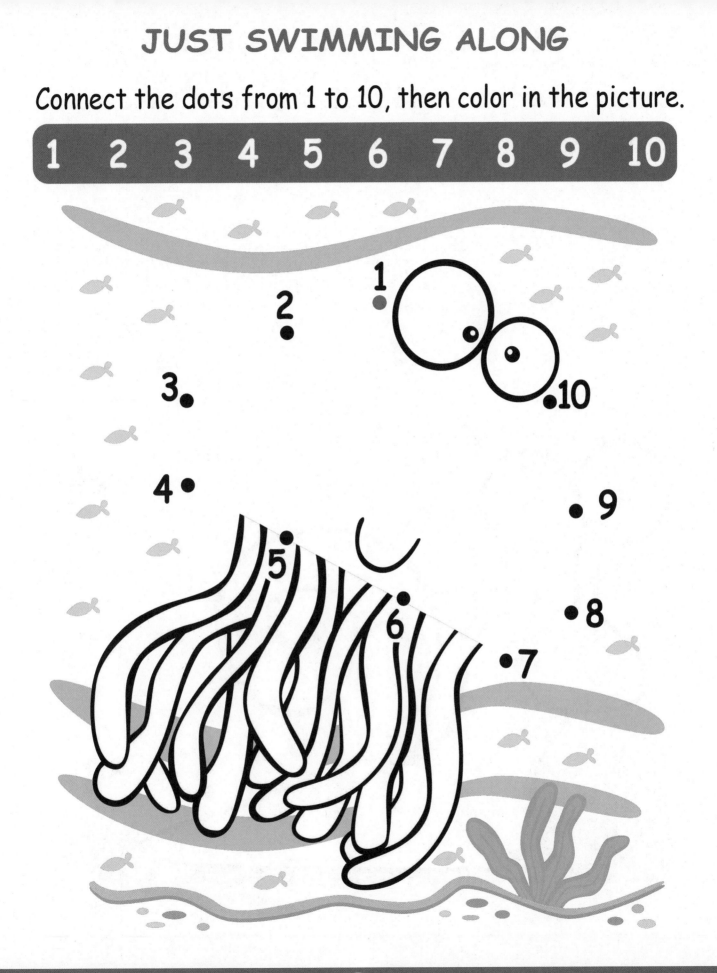

SLOWLY MOVING ALONG

Connect the dots from 1 to 10, then color in the picture.

| 1 | 2 | 3 | 4 | 5 | 6 | 7 | 8 | 9 | 10 |

BREAKFAST TIME

Connect the dots from 1 to 10, then color in the picture.

1 2 3 4 5 6 7 8 9 10

Numbers 0–10

FRUITY NUMBERS 0-10

Trace and write the numbers 0-10.

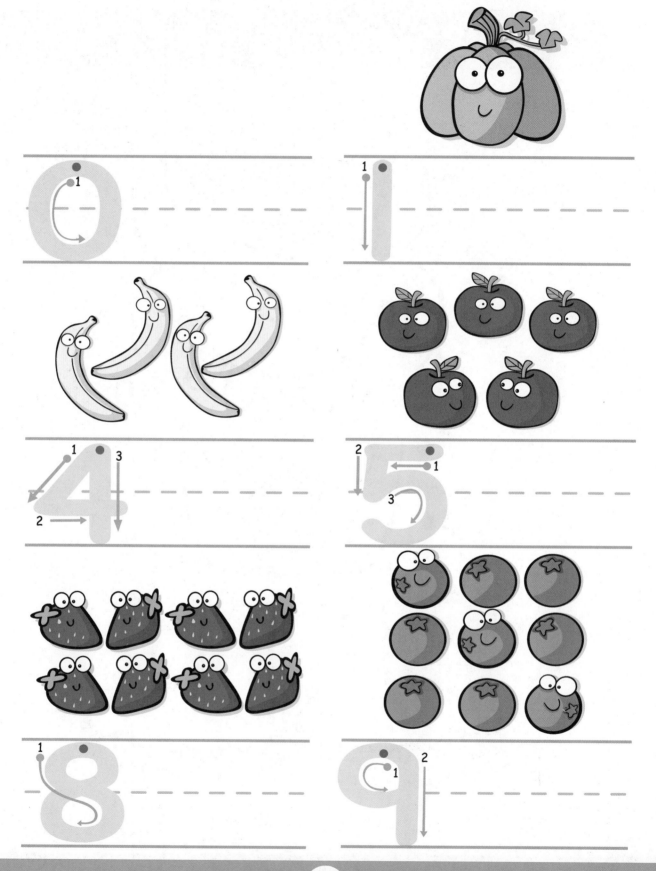

4 is before 5.

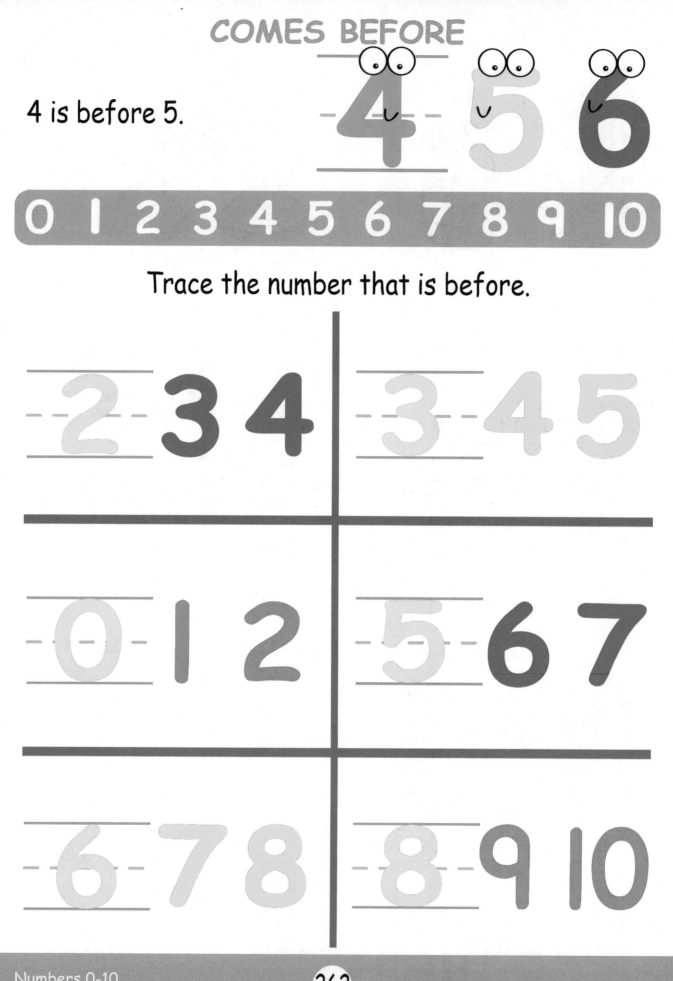

4 5 6

0 1 2 3 4 5 6 7 8 9 10

Trace the number that is before.

2 3 4   3 4 5

0 1 2   5 6 7

6 7 8   8 9 10

IN BETWEEN

3 is between 2 and 4.

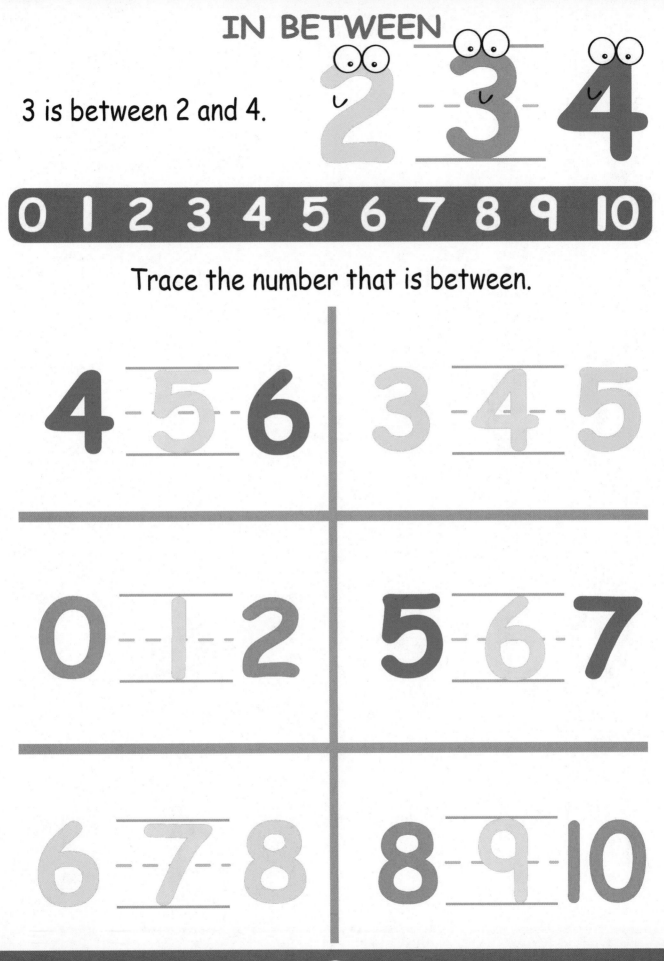

0 1 2 3 4 5 6 7 8 9 10

Trace the number that is between.

4 5 6

3 4 5

0 1 2

5 6 7

6 7 8

8 9 10

Numbers 0-10

COMES AFTER

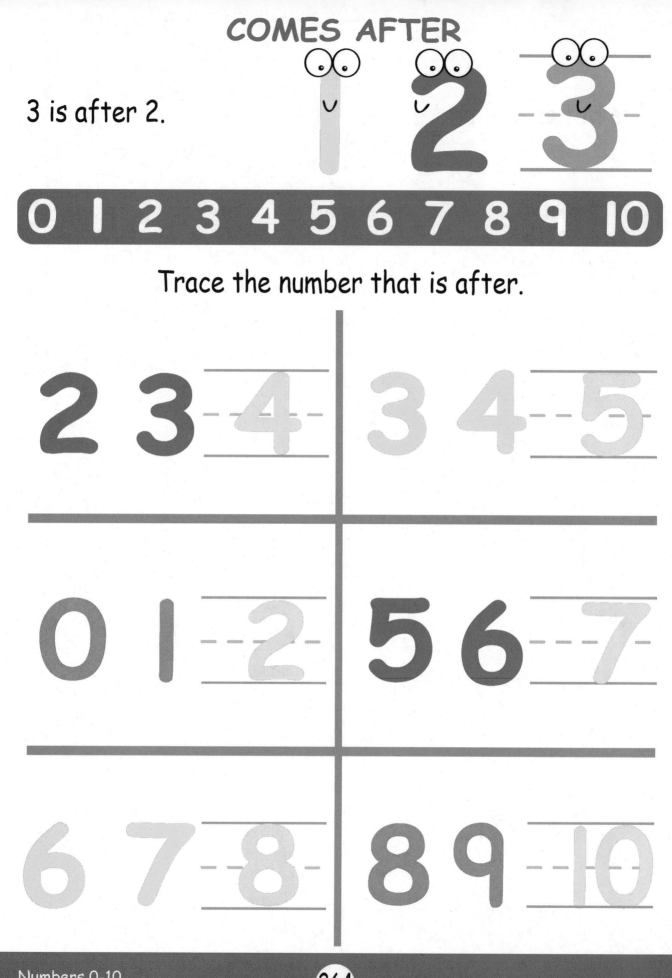

3 is after 2.

1 2 3

0 1 2 3 4 5 6 7 8 9 10

Trace the number that is after.

2 3 4   3 4 5

0 1 2   5 6 7

6 7 8   8 9 10

WHICH HAS THE SAME AMOUNT?

Circle the group on each line that shows the same amount as the first picture.

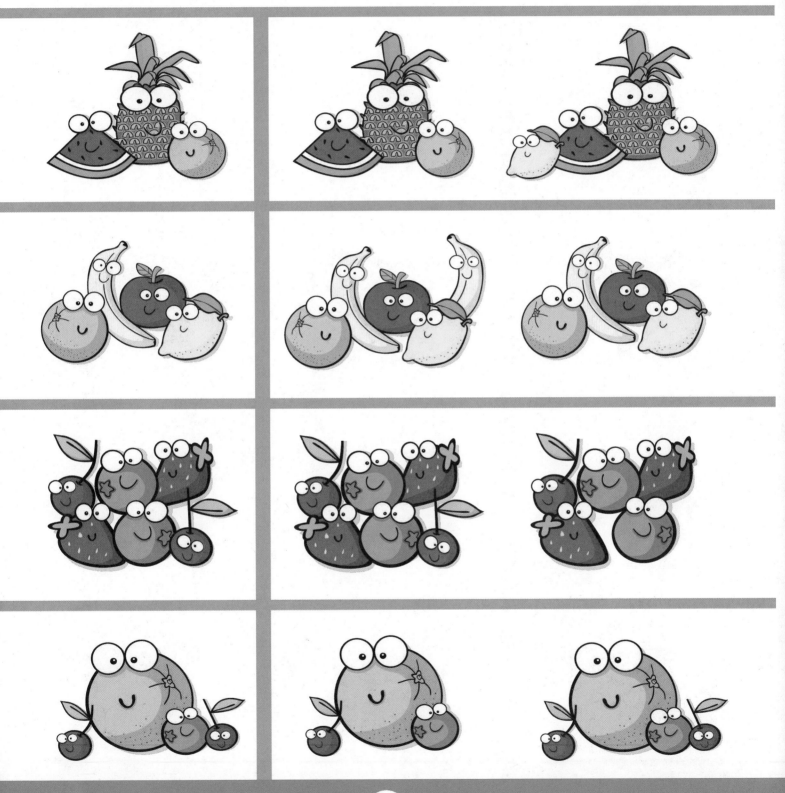

Numbers 0-10

WHICH HAS ONE MORE?

Circle the group on each line that shows one more than in the first picture.

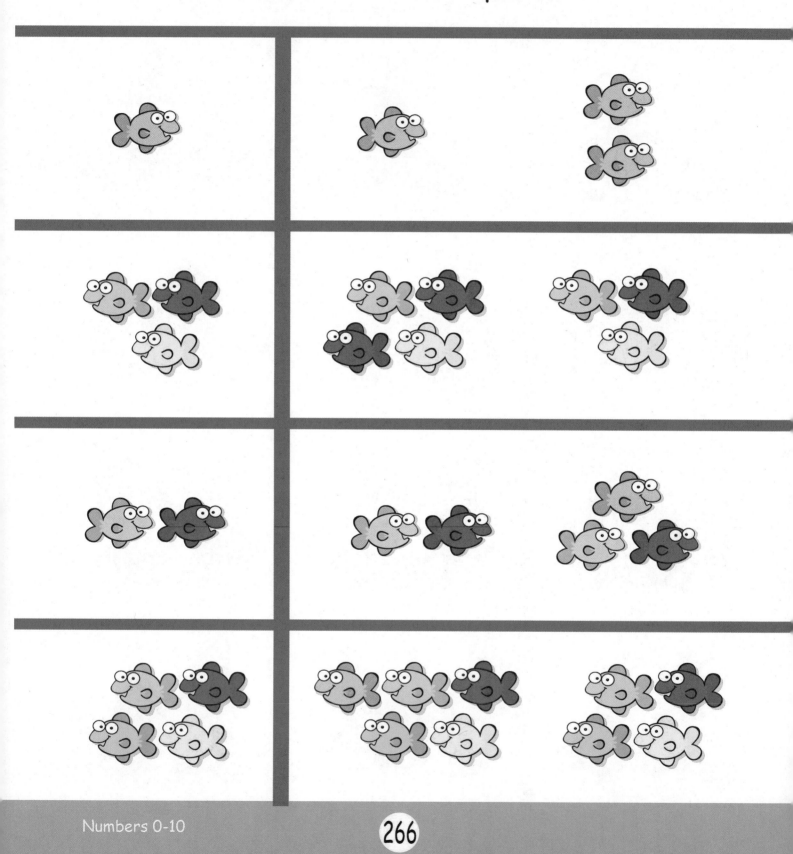

WHICH HAS ONE FEWER?

Circle the group on each line that shows
one fewer than in the first picture.

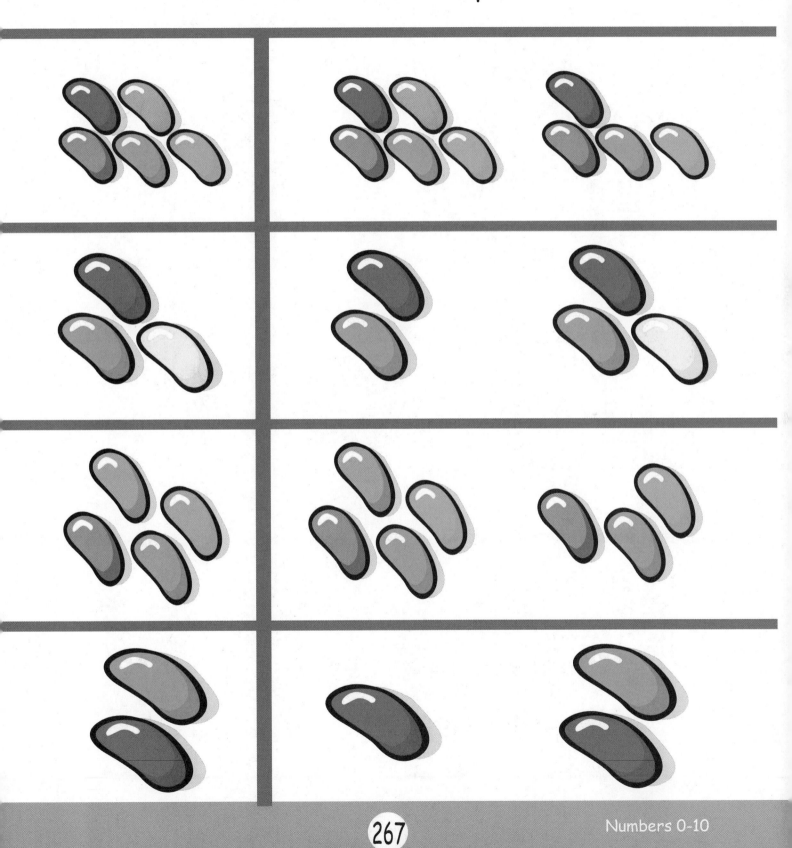

GREATER THAN

Greater means more than.
Circle the group in each row that has more.

FEWER THAN

Fewer means not as many.
Circle the group in each row that has fewer.

Numbers 0-10

THE SAME & DIFFERENT

Circle the picture in each row that is the same as the first one.

THE SAME & DIFFERENT

Circle the picture in each row that is the same as the first one.

ONE IS DIFFERENT

Circle the picture in each row that has something different than the first one.

THE SAME & DIFFERENT

Circle the picture in each row that is different than the first one.

SOMETHING IS NOT RIGHT

Circle the picture in each row that has something missing, then draw the missing parts.

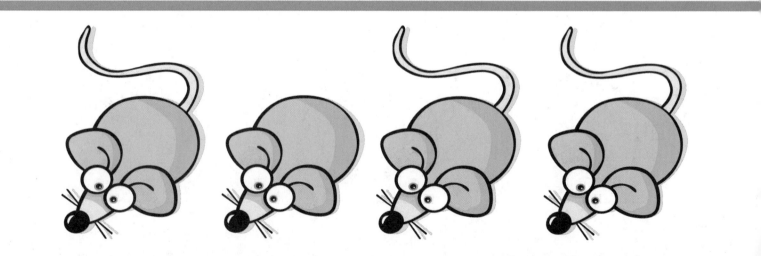

DRAW WHAT'S MISSING

Each of the bees is missing something.
Draw in the missing parts.

Missing Pieces

WHAT IS MISSING?

Draw in what is missing in the picture below.

WHAT IS MISSING?

Draw in what is missing in the picture below.

Missing Pieces

MATCHING BOOTS

Draw lines to match the pairs of boots.

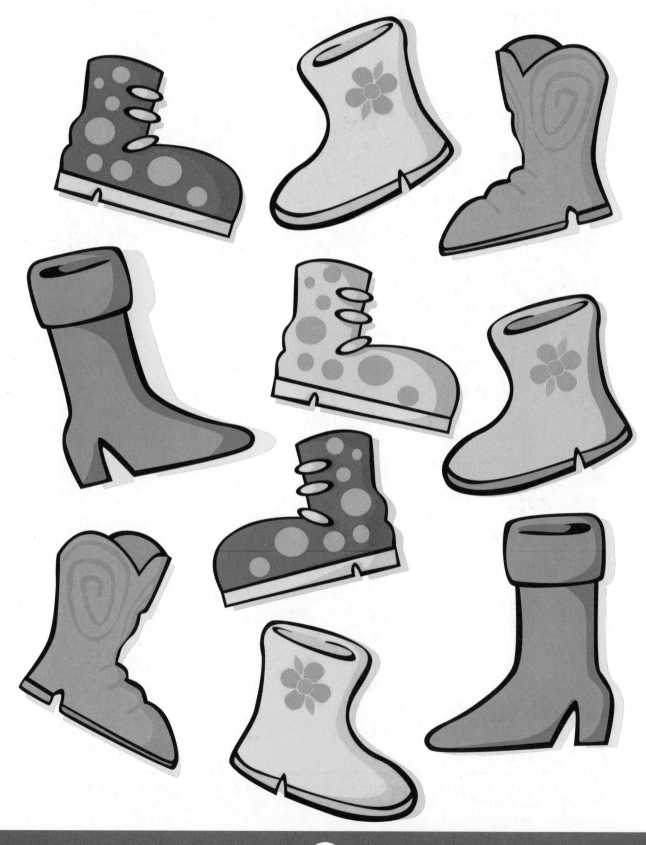

MATCHING SOCKS

Draw lines to match the pairs of socks.

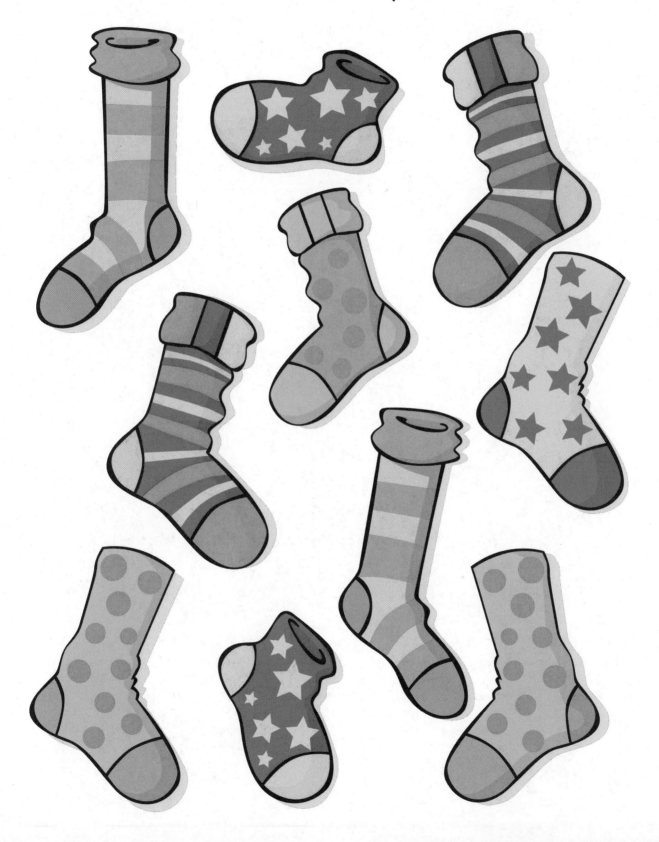

Matching

UNDER THE SEA

Find and circle the pictures in the scene.

AT THE CANDY STORE

Find and circle the pictures in the scene.

IN THE GARDEN

Find and circle the pictures in the scene.

WINTER SQUIRREL PLAY

Find and circle the pictures in the scene.

WHICH BELONG TOGETHER?

Circle the picture in each row that belongs with the first image.

WHICH BELONG TOGETHER?

Circle 2 pictures in each row that belongs with the first image.

Belong Together

WHAT BELONGS IN A TREE?

Circle what belongs in a tree.

LET'S GO GROCERY SHOPPING

Draw a line to the grocery bag the items belong in.

peas

orange

carrot

corn

strawberry

zucchini

pineapple

broccoli

watermelon

Fruits

Vegetables

Belong Together

WHAT DOES NOT BELONG?

Cross out the picture that does not belong in each row.

WHAT DOES NOT BELONG?

Cross out the picture that does not belong in each row.

Does Not Belong

SUMMER & WINTER

Draw lines between the items you wear and the season you wear them in.

SPRING & FALL

Draw lines between the items you see
and the season you see them in.

WHOSE TAIL IS WHOSE?

Draw a line from the pictures below to match the tails at the bottom of the page.

animal   bird   reptile

LOOK VERY CLOSELY!

Look at the monsters until you remember them.
Turn to page 294.

WHO DO YOU REMEMBER SEEING?

Circle the monsters you remember seeing on page 293.

HOW WOULD YOU FEEL?

Draw the face on the monsters to show the way you would feel.

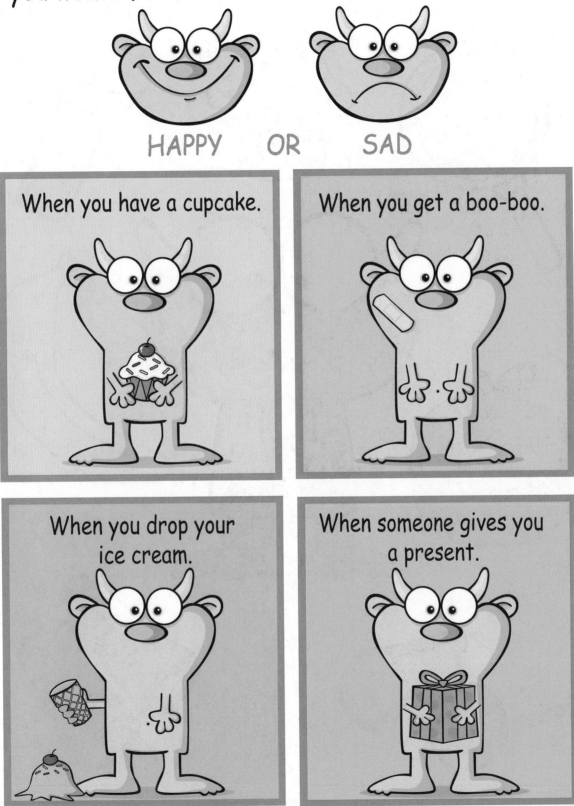

HAPPY   OR   SAD

When you have a cupcake.

When you get a boo-boo.

When you drop your ice cream.

When someone gives you a present.

Emotions

WHAT HELPS YOU SEE?

Circle the items that help you see.

WHAT CAN YOU TASTE?

Circle the items that you can taste.

WHAT CAN YOU SMELL?

Circle the items that you can smell.

WHAT CAN YOU HEAR?

Circle the pictures that make a noise.

WHAT CAN YOU TOUCH?

Circle the items that you can touch.

WINTER FUN

Circle the things you would use in the winter.

SUMMER FUN

Circle the things you would use in the summer.

EATING HEALTHY

Name the foods in each group,
then circle your favorites.

FRUITS

nuts

banana

apple   blueberries

orange

rice

tofu

egg

PROTEINS

cheese

DAIRY

strawberry

yogurt

cereal

GRAINS

milk

fish

butter

pasta

chicken

zucchini

corn

bread

carrot

peas

broccoli

mushroom   VEGETABLES

Nutrition

FARM DELIVERY

Help the farmer get her produce to the market.

Community Map

IN OUR COMMUNITY

Draw a line between the workers in our community and the items they use to do their jobs.

OPPOSITES

Draw lines to match up the opposites.

soft

happy

cold

hard

sad

hot

OPPOSITES

Draw lines to match up the opposites.

stop

back

front

day

night

go

OPPOSITES

Draw lines to match up the opposites.

big

awake

fast

little

asleep

slow

SILLY FARM

Circle 5 silly things in this picture.

SILLY BUG CITY

Circle 5 silly things in this picture.

Visual Distinction

SILLY UNDERWATER

Circle 5 silly things in this picture.

WHAT HAPPENS NEXT?

Look at the pictures on the left and draw a line to what happens next on the right.

Cause & Effect

WHAT HAPPENED BEFORE?

Look at the pictures on the left and draw a line to what happened before on the right.

WHAT HAPPENED BEFORE?

Look at the pictures on the left and draw a line to what happened before on the right.

Cause & Effect

IN OUR TREEHOUSE

Find and circle the pictures in the scene.

AT THE BAKERY

Find and circle the pictures in the scene.

Search & Find

AT THE TOY STORE

Find and circle the pictures in the scene.

THE BIRTHDAY PARTY

Find and circle the pictures in the scene.

YOU'RE AWESOME

Congratulations

Name

has completed the
The Awesome Activity Book for Curious Kids
from
Skyhorse Publishing Inc.

ALSO AVAILABLE FROM RACEHORSE FOR YOUNG READERS:

ALSO AVAILABLE FROM RACEHORSE FOR YOUNG READERS: